Praise for *Choices and Illusions*

"Read this book! We are living at a time when people are searching for answers to fundamental questions in their lives. This book can be, if applied, a road map to personal enlightenment and empowerment. I believe it can 'tune in' the frequency you are currently operating on. More important, it helps you see that you can manifest change."

— John Edward, psychic medium and author of
After Life and *Understanding Your Angels and Meeting Your Guides*

*"**Choices and Illusions** is a smart, practical book by a grand master of the mind. If you want to get out of the box of your own thinking, and touch a greater reality, Eldon Taylor can show you how."*

— Joan Borysenko, Ph.D., author of *Your Soul's Compass*
and *Inner Peace for Busy People*

*"**Choices and Illusions** opens our minds to explore inwardly—to explore how our minds work and how to harness our minds to become clear about our purpose in life and the Love that we are."*

— Gerald G. Jampolsky, M.D., author of *Teach Only Love* and
Good-bye to Guilt

"This is an extraordinary and complete overview of mind and consciousness from someone who has been demonstrating it in his life for many years."

— Lynne McTaggart, author of *The Field* and *The Intention Experiment*

*"More and more people are reaching out today in search of answers to life. Sometimes the search is to understand relationships, improve performance, or become successful—unfortunately, most people look outside of themselves for both the answers and the best actions. They excuse themselves with rationalizations. If only the universe would give me a break. If only he or she would change. If only I had been born differently, and so on. If you've found yourself somewhere in life where you don't want to be, then read **Choices and Illusions.**"*

— Marci Shimoff, professional speaker and #1 *New York Times*
best-selling author of *Happy for No Reason, Love for No Reason,*
and *Chicken Soup for the Woman's Soul*

"When you realize just how much of your actions are automatic and how many of your choices are actually made by your subconscious, you understand the illusion we all have lived most of our lives! Eldon Taylor's book **Choices and Illusions** delivers both the path in and the way out to move from where you are to where you want to be, and it does so in straight talk everyone can understand. This book should be required reading for young and old alike!"

— **C. Norman Shealy, M.D., Ph.D.,** author of *Energy Medicine*

"I can see why **Choices and Illusions** became a <u>New York Times</u> bestseller when it was first released—and this revised edition offers so much more. This is the best guidebook to show you how you got where you are and how you can get to where you would rather be. Once again, in his enlightening and compelling style, Eldon Taylor reveals inestimably valuable information to help you achieve the success you seek in any of your goals."

— **Sandra Anne Taylor,** *New York Times* best-selling
author of *Quantum Success*

"Your mind is incredibly powerful. You have been brought to this exact moment in your life by your thoughts. In **Choices and Illusions,** Eldon Taylor offers clear guidelines for changing your life and your choices for the better."

— **Caroline Sutherland,** best-selling author of *The Body Knows*

"**Choices and Illusions** is a valuable addition that many individuals will find accessible and helpful."

— **Steven Halpern,** composer/recording artist and
pioneering sound healer

"Taylor has reached the mind-magic fulcrum by creating a matrix for shifting perceptual reality. A bold work! The extent that consciousness pervaded the landscape of inquiry above life itself is indeed the frontier of evolutionary science."

— **Elaine Smitha,** author of *If You Make the Rules, How Come You're Not Boss?* and host/producer of *Evolving Ideas* radio and TV

"In **Choices and Illusions,** Eldon Taylor takes us on a delightful and provocative odyssey through the corridors of consciousness. Using solid science, practical spirituality, and common sense, he shows that our perceptions can be changed—and, once different, can catalyze dramatic improvements in our health and well-being."

— **Dawson Church, Ph.D.,** author of *The Genie in Your Genes*

*"I thoroughly enjoyed Eldon Taylor's work of wisdom. It will lead
the reader to a glimpse of the 'Open Mind,' which merges
science and spirituality."*

– Vijayendra Pratap, Ph.D., D.Y.P., founder/director of the Yoga Research
Society and the SKY Foundation; director of the yoga program, Jefferson-
Myrna Brind Center of Integrative Medicine; and author of *Beginning Yoga*

"Transformationally insightful and thought provoking, Dr. Eldon Taylor's
Choices and Illusions *examines the most basic assumptions we hold and
take for granted. Dr. Taylor clearly elucidates how our thought patterns and
beliefs impact our realities; shape our futures; and contribute to our self-esteem,
happiness, success, and fulfillment—or to the lack of these desirable qualities.
His fresh perspectives regarding the many assaults we receive from the outside
world daily and how the invisible paradigms we are subject to limit our joy,
personal power, and ability to step into our potential open up an entirely new
world of possibilities for our growth and development. Dr. Taylor is one of
the foremost philosophers of our time, and his book is a great contribution to
empowering our lives and sourcing our magnificence.
I strongly recommend it."*

– Dr. Joe Rubino, CEO, The Center for Personal
Reinvention, and author of *The Self-Esteem Book*

*"I have known and admired Eldon Taylor for over 20 years. When we were
struggling to build America's first National Judo Institute in Colorado, Eldon
called to discuss the psychological progress of our athletes. He volunteered to
visit us at his own expense to create a subliminal audio program for our Judo
champions. We worked out the affirmations with Eldon's help and used the
program a great deal. That audio program was, I believe, an important
factor in our winning first place in America as a team for several years,
securing several spots on the 1992 US Olympic Judo Team,
and Kate Donahoo's fifth place finish in those Olympics.*
"Now I am very excited about Dr. Taylor's new book, **Choices and
Illusions.** *To me, it not only gives the scientific background we need to
understand how subliminal learning takes place, but it also ties our minds
in with the only logical explanation of reality I know. It simply proves to
me again, in a scientific and wonderful way, how our minds are part of
the one reality, and how we are inhibited from realizing that reality by our
conditioning, attitudes, and beliefs. Then the book goes on to let us know
how we can return home to our true nature. I don't believe there is a more
important book on human happiness than* **Choices and Illusions.***"*

– Philip S. Porter, founder, United States Martial Arts Association;
Major, United States Air Force (Retired); United States
Military Academy, West Point, class of 1948

"I think few today would deny the connection between the body and mind—particularly with respect to one's mental and physical well-being. Dr. Taylor has gone into intricate detail to show some of the deeply hidden ways in which we 'create' our successes and disappointments in life. But most of all, he shares how we might all consciously design the life we truly desire and proceed to achieve it. En route, he points out that we are likely to experience 'tests'—and, in fact, a never-ending series of tests that are the source of our continuing learning and growth. And somewhere along this journey—independent of age—he suggests we quite naturally discover a deeper dimension of ourselves, the spiritual. Finally, Dr. Taylor points out discovering that wholeness—body, mind, and spirit—within ourselves is the true source of happiness. Along this journey of continually discovering happiness, he discusses the detailed workings of the mind and suggests ways we can transform our deeply ingrained fears into empowering, motivating beliefs about ourselves. The result is a book that will not only change _your_ perspective of life, but also result in a deeper understanding, empathy, and compassion for others. I highly recommend **Choices and Illusions**—it's a must read!"

— **William A. Guillory, Ph.D.**, founder of Innovations Consulting and author of several books, including *The Living Organization: Spirituality in the Workplace*

"Why do we have such a difficult time making and sticking with changes we wish to incorporate in our lives? A challenging question, indeed, and it's been addressed by many self-help gurus and spiritual groups. Although well intentioned, few actually succeed in 'helping' others to help themselves. They inspire for a brief moment, but the changes rarely kick in and stay put! "**Choices and Illusions** explains not only why this phenomenon happens repeatedly, but actually provides a pathway around the subconscious saboteur that impedes one's progress. Dr. Eldon Taylor, a well-respected expert in the field of subliminal communication, leads the reader into a place of simplified understanding of the discipline that brings an end to the war between the heart and the head, between spirit and science. In a time when we're desperately seeking a balance between the dualities in our lives, **Choices and Illusions** provides a true recipe for success, sans the confusion which often accompanies the arrogance of intellectualism. There isn't a person alive who wouldn't benefit from this read!"

— **Angelina Heart,** author of *The Teaching of Little Crow*, Heart Flame Publishing

CHOICES
AND
ILLUSIONS

ALSO BY ELDON TAYLOR

CHANGE WITHOUT THINKING (3-DVD set)*

EXCLUSIVELY FABRICATED ILLUSIONS

*I BELIEVE: When What You Believe Matters!**

JUST BE: A Little Cowboy Philosophy

LITTLE BLACK BOOK

*MIND PROGRAMMING: From Persuasion and Brainwashing to Self-Help and Practical Metaphysics**

SELF-HYPNOSIS AND SUBLIMINAL TECHNOLOGY: A How-To Guide for Personal-Empowerment Tools You Can Use Anywhere! (book-with-CD)*

SIMPLE THINGS AND SIMPLE THOUGHTS

SUBLIMINAL COMMUNICATION: Emperor's Clothes or Panacea?

SUBLIMINAL LEARNING: An Eclectic Approach

SUBLIMINAL TECHNOLOGY: Unlocking the Power of Your Own Mind

THINKING WITHOUT THINKING: Who's in Control of Your Mind?

*WHAT DOES THAT MEAN? Exploring Mind, Meaning, and Mysteries**

*WHAT IF? The Challenge of Self-Realization**

WELLNESS: Just a State of Mind?

Plus hundreds of audio and video programs in multiple languages

*Available from Hay House

Please visit:

Hay House USA: **www.hayhouse.com**®
Hay House Australia: **www.hayhouse.com.au**
Hay House UK: **www.hayhouse.co.uk**
Hay House South Africa: **www.hayhouse.co.za**
Hay House India: **www.hayhouse.co.in**

CHOICES
AND
ILLUSIONS

**How Did I Get Where I Am,
and How Do I Get Where I Want to Be?**

Eldon Taylor

HAY HOUSE, INC.
Carlsbad, California • New York City
London • Sydney • Johannesburg
Vancouver • Hong Kong • New Delhi

Published and distributed in the United States by: Hay House, Inc.: www.hay house.com® • *Published and distributed in Australia by:* Hay House Australia Pty. Ltd.: www.hayhouse.com.au • *Published and distributed in the United Kingdom by:* Hay House UK, Ltd.: www.hayhouse.co.uk • *Published and distributed in the Republic of South Africa by:* Hay House SA (Pty), Ltd.: www.hayhouse.co.za • *Distributed in Canada by:* Raincoast: www.raincoast.com • *Published in India by:* Hay House Publishers India: www.hayhouse.co.in

Cover design: Julie Davison • *Interior design:* Nick C. Welch

Library of Congress Cataloging-in-Publication Data

Taylor, Eldon.
  Choices and illusions : how did I get where I am, and how do I get where I want to be? / Eldon Taylor.
     pages cm
     ISBN 978-1-4019-4338-7 (hardcover : alk. paper) 1. Success--Psychic aspects. 2. Choice (Psychology) 3. Self-perception. I. Title.
  BF1045.S83T38 2013
  158.1--dc23
                                    2013013819

Hardcover ISBN: 978-1-4019-4338-7

16 15 14 13   4 3 2 1
1st printing, revised edition, September 2013

Printed in the United States of America

*To the One Source, which created all and
with which we are intricately interconnected—
which includes you. And to three special
aspects of that One Source:
Roy, the wind beneath my wings;
Lois, who made sure the dream lived on;
and Ravinder, who taught me the meaning of love.*

CONTENTS

FOREWORD

I lay back on the couch after finishing this book, and I closed my eyes.

At first I did not know why I had such a strong desire to read it again and to keep it on the nightstand close to me. Then I understood.

What every cell of my body was now experiencing was a new, powerful energy—revitalizing, rejuvenating, and inviting me to start taking action immediately. It was the energy that only hope can bring.

Yes, what this book brings to the reader is hope. It represents the life-saving ring thrown from an unexpected boat in the middle of the ocean to an exhausted swimmer who has lost hope of reaching the shore. It is the road back to the civilized world that an explorer, lost in an unfriendly jungle, suddenly discovers. It is the island with a landing field that a pilot of a plane almost out of fuel suddenly sees through the clouds above a rough ocean.

This book offers the reader not only a powerful insight into how the subconscious mind is dictating human behavior, but also the solution to regaining control of our existence on this planet.

And this is where the book stands out. We are finally able to acquire an understanding of why different things happen to us in our lifetime and also how to start changing our destiny, no matter how far away we are from this knowing.

It is a book for all, the initiated as well as those still under the power of the illusions of this life.

It is a book designed to awaken the human consciousness.

What a wonderful relief to know that it is never too late to start changing, and also to know that we are always in full control of this process!

In my career as a neurologist, nothing produced a more dramatic effect on my patients' state of mind and their ability to recover from any condition than the sudden realization that they are themselves capable of influencing their own health, that they themselves are in the driver's seat, not the doctor.

After reading this book, the spiritualists will definitely claim Dr. Eldon Taylor as one of their own.

At the same time, the numerous scientific studies proving the validity of his approach in mind training with InnerTalk, done by reputable researchers, will place Dr. Taylor among scientists.

So, the only possible conclusion is that Dr. Taylor is both a scientist and a spiritualist.

By bridging these fields, he becomes a pioneer in what I believe could be considered the science of spirituality.

Last but definitely not least, Dr. Taylor is a humanitarian. Those who have become acquainted with his work over the years easily realize that it is inspired by love, an unconditional love for a human race at a crossroads and desperately needing to redefine itself in order to survive. His entire work and life are dedicated to this purpose.

I am firmly convinced that as long as people like Dr. Taylor exist, there is still hope for our planet to be saved and for our civilization to continue its progress toward enlightenment.

— **Cristian Enescu, M.D.**

◉◉◉◉◉◉

PREFACE

There is only one purpose to this work. This became very clear to me the other morning while I was acknowledging and giving thanks for all the blessings in my life. As I thought of many just from the day before, I remembered two small house martins playing with me while I watered the family's strawberry bed. One of the birds actually landed on the coffee cup in my left hand. The other bird sat less than six inches directly above my head on a branch of the elm tree that overhangs this garden. As if teasing me, they both then darted in and out of the stream of water from the garden hose held in my other hand. The entire scene was simply magical. The two birds apparently had no fear of me. I enjoyed their frolic and returned their teasing with an occasional movement of the stream of water as they flew through it to land on a low-hanging branch.

For a few moments the birds and I knew no boundaries in terms of the traditional fear-laden relationship that all too often abides between man and nature. I even mused that it would have been something like this if the story of the Garden of Eden were to be drawn out in detail. There was a special sort of oneness—oneness from the One Source, the oneness that goes beyond the common denominator of atoms and molecules shared by all; it was the oneness of consciousness that abides in peace, balance, and harmony—harmony with all.

This vision in my mind of the events with two small birds and my feeling of happiness and joy that I believe was shared by the birds gives rise to the meaning and purpose behind this book. To the realization of your birthright, may you find this work worthy of your time and energy.

Be well and happy,
Eldon

◦◉◦◉◦◉◦

INTRODUCTION TO
THE FIRST EDITION

"There has to be another way" is a popular motto in politics and in life. We get to this slogan when things simply don't work as well as we want them to. In our personal lives, we may discover that life is flying by and, as with Little Black Sambo's tiger, we are just going in endless circles. Abraham Maslow believed that sooner or later mature individuals come to a point where the question becomes something similar to, "Is that all there is?" The principle labeled by Maslow as "self-actualization" then becomes important.

What is self-actualization? Like success, it can be many different things to different people. Like success, it is a level of satisfaction that arises from within ourselves: a sense of somehow making a difference to someone, a sense that our life has had purpose and meaning—that in some way or another, our life has been worth living.

I have heard so-called motivational gurus suggest that success is all about money and power. I have heard them state such things as "Spirituality is something you do when you get old." I don't believe that. For me, life is about a deeper meaning. Each of us has unique talents and abilities. My experience suggests that most fail to recognize their own birthright and find themselves trapped by beliefs that limit their personal possibilities. For me, life is about using those talents and abilities to the highest while serving an inner calling to make a difference with our lives.

It has often been stated that insanity is doing the same thing over and over while expecting a different outcome. To avoid this definition of insanity, sometimes it's necessary to convolute our models and reexamine our possibilities. This book is designed to assist and facilitate that alternative way of thinking for all who choose to read it.

I enjoy assembling puzzles. The most challenging puzzles require assembling small pieces into larger pieces before linking all the pieces in a complete picture. In a way, it's necessary to build the alternatives offered in this book in the same way. At times it may seem to you that the subject at hand is either a tangential path or a digression. I have therefore used my own story to weave together the many parts into a coherent whole.

This work is a road map for the person who is seeking a better way. In it I suggest ideas, introduce research, and review data—all in a manner designed to lead you on a quest for your potential and excellence. It is my sincere hope that this little book opens the door for you and encourages you to step through it. Enjoy your journey.

◉◉◉◉◉◉

INTRODUCTION TO THE SECOND EDITION

The power of the mind has always fascinated me, and I have been studying ways to access and enhance this inner force for more than 25 years.

Eight years ago I was invited to speak at the Putra Medical Centre in Malaysia about "Change Without Thinking." This full-day presentation was eventually turned into a book, the first edition of *Choices and Illusions*. No one was more surprised than I was when it became a *New York Times* bestseller. I could only conclude that there are many people out there who are searching for answers to the same questions.

Since *Choices* was written, I have written a number of additional books, all approaching the same issue from very different perspectives. Some individuals have questioned my varying angles of approach, not understanding the connection between the miraculous stories covered in *What Does That Mean?: Exploring Mind, Meaning, and Mysteries* and the darker side of brainwashing, as covered in the first section of *Mind Programming*. A number of people threw their hands up in disgust at *What If?*, choosing to believe that this book was designed to change their minds rather than open them up to vast new possibilities. Everyone loved *I Believe,* but questions still were raised regarding the practical applications.

Choices and Illusions was always designed to be the overall package of ideas, with these other books considering different topics in much greater depth. I therefore decided to prepare a revised edition of *Choices* in order to explain all of these aspects more fully, clearly demonstrating the importance of integrating them into one complete whole. My lifetime of work shows me clearly that the only way you can possibly discover your true self and become the person you were meant to be—free of self-destructive patterns and ideas—is by doing the following:

1. Understanding the way your mind works;

2. Becoming fully aware of the 24/7 effort made by many to program your thinking;

3. Being able to look at yourself and your ideas with fresh eyes, questioning all of your beliefs;

4. Reviewing the full experience of your own life and those of your friends and family members so you can stand back and see the big picture; and

5. Knowing the full potential of your mind and the importance of controlling your inner beliefs to thereby create a goal and a pathway to it.

It is with this aim in mind that I offer you this revised edition of *Choices and Illusions.* Although I do refer to my other books throughout, this is only for the benefit of those who wish to explore certain areas in greater depth. My aim has always been to keep *Choices* as a complete work in its own right; therefore, I have provided within these pages all of the information I believe that you will need to put yourself firmly on the path of reaching your own highest potential.

CHAPTER 1

◦◈◦◈◦◈◦

Choices and Illusions

*"The intuitive mind is a sacred gift and the rational mind
is a faithful servant. We have created a society that
honors the servant and has forgotten the gift."*

— Albert Einstein

Paraphrased, J. Krishnamurti said, "Choice is an illusion. Do I do this—do I do that—all of this is confusion. I can only choose when I'm confused. When I know clearly, there is no choice."[1] Thirty years ago, Benjamin Libet showed that there is activity in the subconscious milliseconds before a conscious thought occurs. In other words, our so-called conscious thoughts are given to us by our subconscious.[2] Indeed, we have recently learned that the subconscious, or unconscious—here I use these terms as synonyms—makes 90 percent of our decisions for us. In fact, an fMRI technician can know what we will decide many seconds before we know our own decision simply by watching the brain in real time. That fact alone should give every thinking person pause to reconsider the content of his or her own mind.[3]

What Is Wrong?

People everywhere want to know how to improve their lives. Typically they believe that if they had more money, more power, more success, and better relationships, then they would be happy. Because of such beliefs, the world is full of fixers. There is a motivational guru on every corner, and there is no shortage of individuals waiting to spend their time and money on learning the "secrets to success." In a sense, I'm no different; however, after more than 30 years of working with those who are in emotional distress, people seeking inner peace, athletes looking to win gold medals, sports organizations striving to win championships, ordinary folks trying to find a place in this world, and so on, I have learned this: the model is all wrong!

What is wrong with more money or better relationships? Nothing! Then what do I mean that the model is wrong? The model is upside down, and it needs to be inverted—but before I can explain what I mean, it is necessary to digress a bit.

An Interdependent State of Being

In the beginning was the big bang. According to preeminent physicist Stephen W. Hawking, before the world of shoes and ships and sealing wax, there existed only singularity. Somehow singularity divided itself, and *bang*—everything was born. Out of something we can only think of as super-super-compressed nothing—everything! To say this with a slightly different twist, from no thing came every thing. Based on the creation stories of most major religions, in the beginning the Source, or Creator, reflected upon itself (typically Himself) and divided Himself, creating everything. Notice that the words *singularity* and *Creator* are only reference points for a perspective. That is, if one is inclined to find a *Grand Organizing Designer* (GOD), then the chosen noun *Creator* declares so; and if one tends toward avoiding such an agency, the noun *singularity* declares so. In other words, only one word separates these initial views of creation. Be that as it may, my point is that from the same source came everything. As such, everything is necessarily interrelated and interdependent. I will discuss this more fully later, but for now I am asserting (and I am not the first to do so) that you, your neighbor, and the atoms in your pet are all participating in an interdependent state of being with the whole of the universe.

The Chicken People

All right, let's use a little imagination and begin with the beginning. Please just assume for a moment that instead of being human, you are actually a chicken. Not just any chicken, but a special, advanced species of chicken. Your species has a history of great thinkers. They have struggled with the first question, "Where did I come from?" Many philosophers have used your language to confuse everything: "Which came first, the chicken or the egg?" Your science-minded best thinkers have insisted that the question was irrelevant, stating flatly that you originated from the evolution of a single cell built from molecular building blocks, ever adapting to the conditions of your physical environment, despite the fact that the very building materials needed to construct the first DNA molecule did not exist—and only DNA can create DNA.[4] Many of your psychologists have advanced the general opinion that your basic need for survival, your drive mechanisms—fight, flight, feeding, and fornication—underlie most behavior. Indeed, survival-of-the-fittest mechanisms, basic drives necessary for the propagation of your species, explain advanced theories defining behavior in ways even psychologists disagree over. Some of your metaphysical teachers are preaching a theory of imperfection and an earth age of just a few thousand years, despite overwhelming evidence to the contrary. According to this theory, chickens could have been created perfectly, but they were not. They were made to suffer, and the more they suffered and the better they suffered, the more likely they were to be saved, or go to chicken heaven. Chicken believers in this paradigm worked to convert other chickens to their belief, and believe it or not, many chickens converted. Life sucks and then you die, but when you die, something wonderful happens if you have demonstrated your willingness to be punished for your imperfect deficient self—the self the Creator created.

Your social scientists have quantified group behavior and provided statistical inferences as a result. They are now able to make many predictions about the nature of your social organization, mating habits, and more. Specialized groups have even developed interdisciplinary theories, including those that have mapped your mind and informed you what every corner of it was up to, how it processed information, and so on. Your sciences are truly amazing. Why, even the DNA of your species has been mapped. Such an advanced species you are!

With all this advancement, your chicken yard, or community, still consists of group chicken houses with individual nests. Now let's add just a little extra imagination and use a story to get the full picture of what I'm trying to describe. We'll just imagine a creature raised by the chickens in this story.

The Chicken and the Eagle

It seems a female eagle fell from her nest at a very young age. She wandered until she happened onto a chicken yard, where an older hen adopted and raised her. The chickens taught the eagle the way of chickens. She learned to dig holes and wiggle down into them on hot days to stay cool. She learned to scratch with her talons and soon became valued for her ability to scratch deep into the earth. She learned many things from the chickens, and despite her size was loved by many. She was secure in her chicken house surrounded by her friends and adopted mother. Still, she sometimes felt out of place, uneasy in ways she could not explain, unfulfilled and unnatural. Her friends would reassure her. They would say things like, "Other chickens don't always lay an abundance of eggs" and "Some hens make only a little noise when they do lay an egg." She would confide in her closest friends, and most would reassure her that this was life and she would adjust in time. She needed only to try harder; after all, her biological mother had failed her. This was comforting, for it wasn't her fault—her mother was to blame. Unlike Jonathan Livingston Seagull,[5] there was no great Seagull to teach her otherwise. So, her potential, the possibilities in life, went altogether unknown until one day a male eagle flying overhead spotted her grubbing in the chicken yard.

She is such a grand eagle, he thought, as he descended to speak with her, but one of the chickens caught a glimpse of his shadow and called to the others. The female eagle, who was called Nina, quickly scurried with the chickens to the chicken house, where they hid for the rest of the afternoon. The male eagle was confused but determined.

Days passed before he gained another opportunity. Darting out of the sky with the sun on his face so as not to cast a shadow, he cut off Nina's retreat almost before any in the yard were aware he was approaching. The chickens hid in the chicken house—not one dared to venture out even to see what might be happening to Nina.

Trapped by the male eagle, Nina crouched down in fear, almost paralyzed by her expectation.

"Why are you here?" he asked.

Unable to answer, Nina could only tremble and look down.

"What are you doing here?" he went on. "I have never seen an eagle nesting with chickens, though I've heard such things happen. Have you lost your mind, girl?"

Nina looked up. She suddenly had an idea, for she was a smart chicken. "Did you call me an eagle?" she meekly inquired.

"Of course! You are one. Have you not looked at yourself? Have you not felt the urge to stretch your wings and soar? Have you not felt out of place with these chickens? Do you think those talons were made to dig in the earth? I have watched you for days now. You do everything the chickens do. Why?"

Nina stared in his eyes. They were large and brown. His pupils were dark black and nearly filled his entire eye. He looked as though he could see forever. "You've watched me?" she asked.

"Yes. I've watched you, but I don't understand. You are capable of so much. I could tell you stories for days of adventures and sights that have filled my life—and that should fill yours. You were created with such unlimited potential—you simply don't belong in this yard. You are a beautiful and capable eagle. Can't you see that?"

Nina felt stronger now. Something was wrong with this eagle. *He must have some Messianic complex,* she thought. Imagine his telling her she could soar. Nina said, "So I'm an eagle and I can soar and do things you can show me that I have never done? Is that right?"

"It's in you, girl. Follow your feelings. Be natural. You're not a chicken, I promise."

Nina continued: "So then, since I'm an eagle, you're not going to hurt me."

"Of course not—what nonsense is that?"

"Well, then," Nina confidently added, "show me. Step aside so I could leave if I choose to."

With that, the male eagle stepped out of Nina's path. She seized the opportunity and made the best of her plan, running straight for the chicken house. Once inside she told the chickens how she had outsmarted that dumb old eagle. They all laughed and rewarded her with their chicken appreciation, "You're such a good, smart chicken, Nina!"

The old rooster even spoke nicely to her. "I'm proud of you, Nina—you certainly did outsmart that eagle."

Like Fleas in a Circus

Do you get the moral of the story? Most people have been enculturated to accept and believe certain things that may, and likely do, betray their real potential.

Like the chickens in the chicken yard, we have all been imprinted—the term used by behavioral scientists for the process whereby animals seek to be accepted by imitating their peers. An eagle raised in a chicken yard will behave like a chicken, for example. The first tutorial this story provides leads us to this question:

How many chicken beliefs limit you and alienate you from your potential?

R.D. Laing wrote more than 30 years ago in his book *The Politics of Experience:* "The condition of alienation, of being asleep, of being unconscious, of being out of one's mind, is the condition of the normal man." Alan Watts, in his book *Psychotherapy East and West,* quoted from a speech Carl Jung gave to a group of ministers in 1938: "That I feed the beggar, that I forgive an insult, that I love my enemy in the name of Christ—all these are undoubtedly great virtues. What I do unto the least of my brethren, that I do unto Christ. But what if I should discover that the least amongst them all, the poorest of all the beggars, the most impudent of all the offenders, the very enemy himself—that these are within me, and that I myself stand in need of the alms of my own kindness—that I myself am the enemy that must be loved—what then?"

Let us imagine the human condition programmed with negative expectations. Like fleas in a flea circus, we have been raised to believe that some invisible dome defines who we are, how high we can soar, our basic parameters of life expectancy and health, and so forth—self-imposed limitations that we are totally unaware of, boundaries that we honor despite their unreality and the fact that our sages, geniuses, entrepreneurs, and heroes have all told us to ignore them. But, like our female eagle, we believe we know better or we simply do not know how to pierce those limitations.

The Nine-Dot Matrix

Take a look at the nine stars in Figure 1. Using a pencil or pen, connect the centers of all nine stars with four straight lines without lifting your instrument from the page. Try it, if not with a pencil or pen, then in your mind.

Figure 1

Now turn the page and see how easy it is to connect them with four lines if you do not accept the implied boundary of the stars.

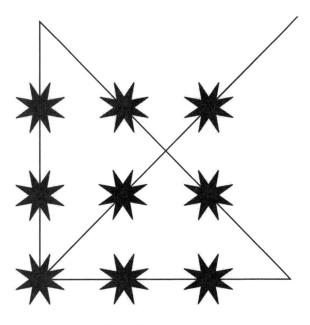

Figure 2

If you are like almost everyone else, extending the lines beyond the so-called boundary of the stars is not something that occurred to you. If it does not come to mind, it is not among your possible choices. Let us illustrate that concept further with a story, because stories stick with us, as do pictures, and are often worth much more than the words that it takes to tell them.

The Flowerpot Story

Imagine that you're visiting New York City for the first time. You're amazed by the skyline—all those immensely tall buildings. You visit a beautiful area of high-rise condominiums. These are truly luxurious condos, all with balconies suspended above the sidewalk. It's a glorious day. The sun is out, and the slight breeze you feel is warm and comforting. The air is unusually fresh, and you're simply walking, taking in the sights and sounds, and enjoying the day to the fullest. It's New York, and you have heard stories about this city, but it's light and bright and pleasant, and you walk on, thinking of all that you'll tell your friends back home.

Suddenly, from the third-floor balcony above you, a flower-pot falls and slams onto your head. The pot is deflected onto the sidewalk and shatters. You're not seriously hurt, but your head is hurting. You feel a bulge rapidly building into a rather large knot. Your scalp has a nasty abrasion that burns when you touch it, and on your hand is a small amount of blood. The suddenness and pain have raised your adrenaline level. That old fight/flight mechanism has kicked in, and the neurochemicals are flowing. Anger begins to rise. Now you have some choices. What would you do?

Let's think about that and explore some possibilities. You could decide to go up to that third-floor condo and shove you know what you know where. You might get there only to discover that the owner is a defensive linebacker for some professional football team and his biceps are larger than your waist. Then you might change your plan.

What else could you do? Some might think of this as an opportunity. "I'll sue this fat cat. Anyone who puts a flowerpot too close to the edge of the balcony railing, just waiting to fall on someone, should be educated. What if it had fallen on a small child or a baby in a buggy passing under the balcony? Suing will be a quickie—they'll settle out of court. That'll teach them to be more careful in the future. Concussion and whiplash—I wonder what those are worth."

What else could you do? Well, some might think the incident was a sign from the gods. It's time to be metaphysical—after all, the blow might have delivered enlightenment. It might even be like one of those lightning strikes in which the person struck gains special metaphysical or parapsychological abilities. Like John Travolta in the movie *Phenomenon,* such a person can do or solve almost anything. It's like instantly acquiring the knowledge of the universe.

What else could you do?

Pyschologist and philosopher William James is often credited with coining the term *pragmatic,* because of his application of the word in philosophy and psychology. What is pragmatic? In our instance, it is simply responding to the stimuli in a manner that works for you. What would work for you? What if you picked up the flower off the hot sidewalk and took it to a florist for repotting? What if you selected a very nice pot, had the plant repotted, and then returned it to the owner with an explanation of why it was in a new pot? You could say something like this: "Your flowerpot fell from your balcony and hit me on the head. The pot smashed against the sidewalk, so I took the flower to the florist and had it repotted for you. Here it is. I hope you like the new pot."

Of all the things you might do, what do you think would make you feel the best? Of all the things you might do, what do you think would change those neurochemicals from fight/flight to growth and pleasure?

Choices

Dr. Bruce Lipton models the body this way: like a government, it has two budgets—one for defense and the other for growth. As such, when the body goes to defense (fight/flight), it cannot grow. When the body is at peace, the budget turns entirely toward growth (optimal health and wellness). If you think of this budget for a moment (we will return to this issue later) and realize that in modern man fight and flight have been replaced with anxiety and depression, it's easy to see that this heightened state of arousal is normal, albeit unhealthy. That is, anxiety and depression are states of alarm (fight/flight), and most people have plenty of stimuli in their everyday lives to keep their bodies aroused in this way.

So, of the choices with respect to our flowerpot story, which choice would serve you best? The answer is obvious. But since it is so obvious, why wasn't it recognized right away? Here is my point. In such a scenario—and believe me, we all have similar scenarios, such as when a person who cuts us off in traffic or pushes into line in front of those who are already waiting—why do we fail to see the obvious and instead choose the lesser?

When the obvious should be so clear, why is it that so many of us fail even to recognize it as an alternative?

Choice? Do I do this, or do I do that? What choice do I have if I cannot see an alternative to the lesser of evils? What, then, do we mean when we believe in free will and choice and yet duck responsibility? As with freedom and democracy, responsibility accompanies choice. Whether with free will or freedom of speech, each of us has a responsibility to become informed and behave intelligently as a result. Then how do we escape the narrow, self-imposed boundaries that predispose our so-called choices?

Before undertaking an answer for that last question, it will be useful to understand a little more about the human condition—how we learn our self-limiting notions and what and how we perceive what we perceive.

◉◈◉◈◉◈◉

CHAPTER 2

ENGINEERING BELIEF

"Belief creates the actual fact."

— WILLIAM JAMES

Imagine what you might do if you learned that faith the size of a mustard seed could move mountains. Just assume for a moment that somehow you discovered this old statement to be based on your belief—your belief in yourself—and that simply believing you could be successful at your goal, whatever it might be, would somehow make that goal attainable. What would you do to cultivate the power of self-belief?

I have spent the greater part of my life studying the mind and consciousness. My investigations have run the gamut from examining evidence for life after death to studying the actions of the mind from a distance. I have developed tools that have assisted people in believing in their own miraculous healing powers and have seen many terminal cancers disappear. I have reported on multiple-personality patients who in one personality have blue eyes, and, at the snap of your fingers, their personality changes along with their eye color—from blue to brown, for example. What has happened here is simply a shift in belief. Think of it this way: in one moment there is Jane, a real stick in the mud, but in the next she becomes Judy, who loves to party and have fun. That change in "memory" of who we are is capable of altering such things as eye color and blood-sugar levels, and even removing tumors from the body as rapidly as the personality changes.[1]

I have written about the many nuances to our mechanistic nature, including psychological characteristics that make us vulnerable to those who plumb the unconscious (such as neuro-marketers and salespeople). I have lectured and shown how the *nucleus accumbens* (a small part of the brain, also sometimes called the "pleasure center") makes roughly 90 percent of our decisions. Now, please understand that this decision-making machine is a part of our unconscious, so I am saying that 90 percent of our choices are made by our unconscious mind. Indeed, as I pointed out earlier, by using fMRI technology, a technician can watch the brain in action as it makes decisions; and what's more, the very same technician will know what you will decide as much as ten seconds in advance of your consciously making the decision. Think on that one!

The unconscious has all manner of mechanisms—such as our response to compliance principles, biases, context-bound definitions, defense strategies, and so forth (I will discuss this more later)—plus it makes almost all of our decisions for us. So are we just products of good old nature/nurture, programmed by the "media-ocracy" that is our environment and thereby not much more than sophisticated automatons performing on cue? Now, I like to ask at this point in a lecture, "What was your last original thought? Truly original?" and usually I get the same answer: *silence.*

Acquired Savantry

Dr. Andrew G. Hodges (a forensic psychiatrist) tells the story of Jason Padgett. After a head injury in 2002, Jason became a mathematical prodigy—a genius. A blow to the head, and his brain's overcompensation for this resulted in Padgett becoming an acquired savant with regard to mathematical ability. Hodges explains how this excited many mathematicians and physicists, because Padgett suddenly had the ability to see every curve, every line, every minute detail of the Pythagorean theorem. As a result, he is the only person today who can draw fractals freehand—others must use the computer. Hodges continues, "[O]ne scientist called him 'superhuman.' But really Padgett is an accidental genius who has tapped into the phenomenal potential in the human mind."[2]

Today the mind has much more to it than the typically defined, so-called conscious, preconscious, subconscious, unconscious, collective unconscious, and/or derivatives thereof. Indeed, we have what Sigmund Freud called the thinking unconscious evidenced; what Malcolm Gladwell identified in his book *Blink* as the "accidental genius"[3] and who, as pointed out by Hodges, has tapped into the genius of the human mind; and what forensic profilers now refer to as the super intelligence.[4] The super intelligence is that part of our mind/brain that must tell the truth, and therefore is an outcropping, I suppose, of what Freud thought of as the superego. Ultimately, this is behind the well-known Freudian slips. The "dazzling new unconscious" is that aspect that is closest to what we generally think of as intuition, but is also much more than that. For example, Gladwell offers as one of his many examples the story of the fire chief who, on joining his men on the floor of a fire, immediately recognizes something he cannot articulate but which informs him of an urgent danger, and he suddenly orders everyone off the floor immediately. Seconds later the entire floor collapses.

Reclaim Your Thoughts

Most people have been lulled into thinking about their lives, their minds, the real power within them, as shallow and limited in ways that simply are false to facts. Still, even those who have come to understand that the limitations are largely self-imposed do nothing more than parrot those words. So, what if you learned of the true power of your belief and discovered that it was invested incorrectly? Instead of believing in yourself, you believed in the swell of mis- and disinformation that abounds everywhere, including in our sciences, and that this was the cause of many of the difficulties you have experienced in life. What if you also learned that you could repattern that subconscious programming— actually changing the information in the subconscious so that it was more consistent with your genuine desires? Would you want to do so? Well, the truth is that you can.

In the computer sciences is an old acronym, GIGO—meaning garbage in, garbage out. The way to end self-destructive patterns, overcome doubt and fear, maintain health and optimism, and so much more rests in the subconscious programming. I have seen the power of hypnosis and subliminal communication modify those unconscious beliefs, and the results are nothing short of astounding. So the question is simple. If you could really take control, find that mustard seed within, would you? If you relate at all to the story of Nina the eagle, then your mustard seed has yet to blossom. Let's see if we can unpack all of this a bit more and set out on a path with the tools for opening up to your own awesome possibilities.

CHAPTER 3

◉◈◉◈◉◈◉

THE FULL POWER OF YOUR BELIEFS

*"It's the repetition of affirmations that leads to belief.
And once that belief becomes a deep conviction,
things begin to happen."*

— ATTRIBUTED TO MUHAMMAD ALI

In all my years of teaching people about the power of the mind, I have yet to meet someone who truly grasps this idea in its entirety. It is for this reason I wrote *I Believe,* so that I could reveal the many ways our inner beliefs affect our life experience. To quote briefly from that book:

> What would you say if I told you that belief influences almost everything in your life, from your DNA[1] to the operation of your endocrine and immune systems, from your emotional well-being to the stability of your moods and attitudes, from your relationships with others to your relationship with yourself—in short, literally every aspect of life? Let me explore that question and in the process share some facts with you. . . .
>
> Thinking, or belief, directly influences the human body. The physical effects of placebos are just one piece of evidence for this claim. It's well known that placebos have healed such incurable health conditions as terminal

cancer.[2] In one case, orange-size tumors that filled a man's upper body disappeared when he was given a so-called cure. In a matter of three days, this patient went from gasping for every breath to bouncing around his hospital room, teasing the nursing staff. . . .[3]

There are many documented reports of miraculous recoveries at the hands of faith healers. Are they further examples of the power of the mind/belief/consciousness? One such miracle worker has been visited by thousands of people from around the world who were previously diagnosed as terminally ill and have come away healed. This miracle worker is João Teixeira de Faria, the man the people of Brazil affectionately call "João de Deus" or "John of God." Qualified professional medical experts have witnessed many of these cases, and the cures are documented. Indeed, a quick Google search for *John of God* will give you weeks of reading material."[4]

The Web of Beliefs

Our life beliefs are like a giant spiderweb. There is no such thing as a stand-alone belief. They are all intricately interlaced and wound into one another in ways that are amazing even to the professional analyst. Even our dissonant beliefs are connected at some level, despite the fact that they are mutually exclusive in nature. We may well believe, for instance, that prosperity will bring us happiness and at the same time hold a deep-seated belief that the love of money is the root of evil. We need not look far in our society to find living proof of this precise example. Take, for instance, the number of individuals who seek to penalize the new millionaire by taking a large portion of his success in taxes, and at the same time aspire to become millionaires themselves. I have led many seminars in which I've asked, "How many of you would like to make a million dollars this year?" and without exception every hand in the house is raised. I have also asked many of these very same people how they would like to pay 50 percent or more of their income in taxes—federal, state, gas, highway, sin taxes on such things as butter and alcohol, and the like? Again, they are unanimous in their response: "*No*—that's unfair!" Yet this is exactly what this same group of people finds fair when framing the question about raising taxes to balance our national budget and meet our social needs.

Beliefs weave together in ways that often blind us. We have beliefs about what a singer should look like, so when Susan Boyle of *Britain's Got Talent* appeared in her disheveled best, the room filled with laughter and even a jeer or two. Judges looked at one another and rolled their eyes, and yet when the woman opened her mouth and began to sing, the most mellifluous of sounds came forth. Stop and ask yourself, why is it we think a singer should look a certain way? What is this belief, and how does it betray us?

Our life beliefs can dictate everything from our relative successes to the way in which we interact with the physical world. I remember well the Sir Roger Bannister story. Bannister declared that he was going to break the unbreakable four-minute mile. He was told by all the experts, including physiologists, that his goal was not only unreachable but physically impossible. Indeed, there are stories of how the Greeks chased runners with wild animals in their attempt to run a mile in a faster time, and all to no avail. Not possible—and yet, "On May 6, 1954, he was a 6-foot-1, 25-year-old medical student at Oxford, running on the university's track at Iffley Road before a meager crowd of 1,000, most of them students." By the end of the day, the four-minute-mile barrier had been smashed. The newly broken psychological barrier led to numerous runners breaking the same record in the next couple of years. Indeed, John Landy ran the mile 46 days later in Finland, setting a new record with a time of 3:57.9.[5]

Beliefs Dictate Reality

The bottom line is this: If you think you'll fail, you will. If you think you know it all, then you are incapable of learning. If you think that 40 or 50 is old, then when you reach that age, your belief will predispose your reality. When I think of this, I am reminded of what a friend told me once. I believe he was in his 30s at the time, doing some moonlighting as a disc jockey at parties. One evening he prepared music for a school reunion—a 50th high school reunion. Without thinking much about those who would attend, he did as he usually did and found music from the era of their senior year. Everything was cued and ready to go; the attendees began to arrive; and then my friend realized that they were for the most part limping, hobbling, and dragging along in slow motion as though it hurt to move. The thought flashed through his head, *How many hip or knee replacements are there out there—what kind of music do you play them?* His music had all been planned for dancing!

At this juncture, there was nothing else for him to do but proceed with his playlist. He told me, "Eldon, they limped in and danced out!" The memory of our younger days is often enough to vitalize a hidden energy, and the next thing we know, we are feeling and acting younger in every way. Our beliefs—our thoughts about aging—have been suspended in favor of our memories attached to music (we will cover this in more depth later). For now, when you think of your life beliefs, don't take them too lightly. They may well hold your future in more ways than one.

Before closing this chapter, there's something else that should be said. I recently attended a continuing-education course sponsored by the Institute for Brain Potential, and there were two take away points emphasized in concluding remarks by the presenter, Dr. Kateri McRae. Those two points are worth repeating over and over again. The first, you absolutely can change. It turns out that you can change your personality, your IQ, your habits, and even physical aspects of your brain. You can increase gray matter and more. Second, and of utmost importance, you can only change what you *believe* you can change! Let me say that again: neuroscience, not some mumbo-jumbo lingo, but hard science based on actual observation, says that *you can change only what you believe you can change!* Remember that the next time you tell yourself something is impossible.

CHAPTER 4

◉◉◉◉◉◉

CREATING SELF

"Flatter me, and I may not believe you.
Criticize me, and I may not like you.
Ignore me, and I may not forgive you.
Encourage me, and I may not forget you."

— WILLIAM ARTHUR WARD

Most of us have been enculturated during maturation to accept and believe certain things that may, and likely do, limit our real potential. Like chickens in the chicken yard, we have all been imprinted—just as with Nina (see Chapter 1).

Estimations by many suggest that for every unit (bit) of positive, affirming information one processes, 90 bits or more of negative information are received. In other words, for every time we are praised or reassured, 90 times we are fed the opposite information. As a result, most of us find ourselves trapped in self-limiting beliefs about our abilities, our intelligence, our worth—even our health and happiness. One study showed that belief predicted not only vocation but also cause of death. That study, conducted by Dr. David Phillips at the University of California, San Diego, evaluated the Asian belief in birth signs. In Asia, persons born under a particular sign, such as the Dog, know from that sign what they are good at, and therefore probably what they will do vocationally. The sign also indicates the cause of death—say, cardiac disease. The research showed clearly a positive correlation between belief and events, no matter the lifestyle of the individual. In other words, clean living and self-denial did not keep away cancer if the birth sign suggested that as the cause of death.[1]

Cancer and Beliefs

In the spring of 1991, I conducted a survey among physicians who had consented to permit their patients to use a special experimental subliminal InnerTalk program that I had created for cancer remission. (I will cover this technology in depth later.) The aim of the study was to look at life expectancy in comparison with the actual mortality rates of cancer patients who used the InnerTalk program. The questionnaire went to physicians whose patients had received the program two to four years earlier. The 12 questions were on a scale of 1 to 5:

1. Strongly disagree
2. Disagree
3. Neutral
4. Agree
5. Strongly agree

The 12 questions consisted of four general categories:

1. The patient's attitude toward the disease before the patient used the program.
2. The patient's attitude toward the disease after the patient used the program.
3. The patient's survival and quality of life.
4. How the physician felt about his/her patients believing their health could be affected by the patient's mind.

This survey yielded many interesting findings, including significant remission rates, for 38 percent of the so-called terminal patients were in remission at the conclusion of the study.

Another overwhelming result might surprise you. Of the four categories, which do you think would be the most consistent factor affecting the life expectancy, or remission rate, in the patient? Most people believe that it is the patient's attitude, even though many of those same people would say that a terminal disease such as cancer could not be affected just by changing the patient's attitude. It wasn't the patient's attitude, however, but the physician's attitude that was the most important factor in determining whether the patient lived or died.

If the physician did not believe that the patient's involvement with the InnerTalk program or attitude could affect the cancer, the patient died, regardless of which treatment procedure was used— radiation, chemotherapy, and so on. The person died regardless of his or her own attitude toward the disease or its ultimate outcome. The one determining factor present in virtually every case was the physician's attitude.

Taking into account only those patients whose physicians agreed, to some degree, that the mind played a role in the patient's health, then the survival/remission rate increased to 46 percent. If we look at those physicians who strongly agreed that the mind or attitude of the patient is important to health and/or health care, the survival/remission rate increased to 60 percent. Narrowing the field down even more, where both the patient and the physician tended to believe strongly that the mind played a role in wellness, the rate of survival/remission increased to 100 percent.

Now, this was a very small pilot study; however, to me, it showed clearly that not only is the mind capable of healing the body, but what individuals *believed they were capable of* directly influenced the outcome. This power of "self-belief" was also demonstrated in a landmark research project carried out by Dr. Ellen Langer, in which certain characteristics of aging were reversed.

Belief and Aging

Dr. Langer of Harvard University took "old people" into the countryside, where they were isolated for one week. The participants were exposed to "photographs, newspapers, radio (music and advertising) and discussions that were strictly limited to topics current twenty years earlier. At the end of the week, the members of the group became younger-looking by three years, gained weight, behaved more independently, and could actually hear better." When the "old people" stopped believing they were old and were reimmersed in a younger time frame, then aging was reversed.[2] Flash back to the last chapter and remember, "They limped in and danced out!"

Hopeless and Helpless

Another revealing study that speaks directly to the power of self-belief is one carried out by Dr. Martin Seligman. Although I hate to see animals used in this way, it does reveal some interesting information. In this study, dogs were placed on an electric grid. To begin with, the dog could get up and move to a part of the floor without a grid in order to avoid electric shock. After the grid was expanded to include the entire floor—when there was no escape from the shock—the dogs just gave up. They lay helpless and whimpering, regardless of whether or not an electric current was applied. Their immune and encodocrine systems almost shut down. There appeared to be no hope, so they seemingly gave up wanting to live. One supposition might be that there was no reason to live, no escape, so their mind-set communicated to the body, and the body responded accordingly.[3]

Power of the Media

Every day the media inundates its audience with messages of disease. These messages typically seek to sell some cure or antidote—but to sell the cure, they must first announce or sell the disease. These commercials create belief and expectation. When you tell someone, "Don't touch—the paint is wet," the person usually touches it. When members of the media tell you day after day what will sicken and even kill you, how much death and disease are they creating? I believe that it is actually criminal, or it should be, that disease is sold this way. (I cover this subject in more detail in my book *Self-Hypnosis and Subliminal Technology*.)

The media also provides images of success, ways to dress, what beauty is, and so on. These sell such goods as sports cars, cosmetics, and the like—good for the economy, maybe, but if the image is not exactly aligned with how the viewer sees him- or herself, then the image suggests a lack on the part of the viewer. There is one big subliminal message in advertising: you're deficient in some way, and therefore you need this product.

Movies such as *First Blood* romanticize getting even. Heroes and heroines build images of courage and strength through violent acts against "bad guys." Children copy what they see. Promoters sell it not just through the movies but also through such add-ons as toys. What child has seen *Star Wars* and not wanted a lightsaber like those of the Jedi masters?

Peers, parents, teachers, and others tend to be insensitive. Their words, looks, gestures, and even jokes often make us feel inferior. We all long to be included, wanted, important. All in all, the negative so far outweighs the positive that it is no wonder many people feel as though their real self is trapped in some empty shell while life speeds by, especially since, according to the National Science Foundation, our minds produce as many as 50,000 thoughts each day. Unfortunately, it's easy to become so accustomed to this state of affairs that we celebrate it with bumper stickers and sayings such as "I don't get even—I get evener!" and "TGIF" (this last saying suggests that work is miserable and sets a frame around what we do five days a week, therefore conditioning us to find work distasteful whether it is or it isn't).

Compensation

Compensation is a psychological mechanism identified first by pioneering psychiatrist H. S. Sullivan. When individuals lack confidence and esteem, they often compensate by extracting their worth from another. An unconscious nonsense belief seems to propel them into behavior that ridicules, offends, and hurts others. Physical violence is just another way of acting out pain or fear—not that it's really any different in an emotional sense. The abuses they dish out can be thought of as their own inner insecurities being compensated for by making someone else feel insecure—as they do. It's all a rapid downward spiral that leads to anything but true happiness and success.

Like Nina, the female eagle in Chapter 1, it is easy to outsmart those who may offer an alternative to the known or the comfortable. Small minds condemn what they do not understand. Like Nina, most people do not accept that within themselves is a power that can change all of those self-limiting, self-destructive beliefs, a power that can indeed result in manifesting a person so self-responsible that he or she walks and lives above the fray—in the world but not of the world. This is truly your birthright. Life is not designed to be only struggle.

Mark Twain tells a story in his work *Letters from the Earth*. In the story, the archangels are deciding where to hide God. It is suggested that they hide Him on the moon or deep beneath the surface of the sea, and so forth. Each suggestion, however, eventually leads the archangels to conclude that humankind is too smart for that—sooner or later they would find God. So where do they decide to hide Him? Within every human being—for "the last place mankind will look is within," they conclude.

Within every human being exists a propensity for greatness. The gifts may vary, and the greatness may be manifested in a vast array of alternatives—say, from carpentry to rocket ships—but the gift that gives us true self-respect and lifts the spirit from "same old, same old" resides within. These are not just words or some lofty notion. This potential resides within each one of us—but if so, then why is it so often denied?

The Four Selves

Every individual essentially has a self-representation that is rehearsed and eventually actualized. The process begins by fantasizing at a very early age. We fantasize a script, perhaps similar to one of those from some Hollywood production. We begin rehearsing it, and we either abandon it to take up a new one or practice it until we role-play that script as who we are. Practicing the script sooner or later automates the behavior. Our imprinting environment plays a significant role in the alternative scripts available to us. If parents are uncaring and abusive, so are their children, and so forth. If warmth and friendliness lead to embarrassment, then coldness and aloofness compensate. If honesty gets us into trouble, then deception becomes a defense strategy, and so forth.

It is much more complicated than expressed here, and it is also just this simple. In fact, every one of us divides the self among four essential views of ourselves:

1. Our actual self

2. Our ideal self

3. Our ought-to-be self

4. Our desired self

These categories were originally developed by Jerome L. Singer, professor of psychology at Yale University, to show how the different selves conflict with each other.[4] I will use them differently, as we shall see.

Our Actual Self

Most of us are aware of a so-called actual self. This is the self that has failed in ways we often will not share with others. This is the private self. This self holds the thoughts we wish we did not have, the acts we wish we had not done, our beliefs about our worth, our attractiveness, and so forth. It is the self of our secrets and our ambitions. It is the self that most people try to change in some way or another at some time in their life—perhaps even perpetually.

Our Ideal Self

The actual self pales by comparison to our ideal self. The ideal self is often a construct built by our culture. This self would live a perfect life without error—but therefore without room for growth.

Our Ought-to-Be Self

Then there is our "ought-to-be self." This is the self full of all our learned "shoulds" and "oughts." This self differs from our ideal self in the sense that many of the oughts are not ours—they are the oughts of our culture, our society—but deep down inside they do not belong to us. Sometimes these oughts are the result of rules that make little or no sense to us; sometimes the oughts are of codependent negotiations such as those implied when Mom said such things as, "If you loved me, you would not behave that way," or "If you loved me, you would do what I said," and so forth. Still, even when we recognize the source and the nature of the relationship from which the oughts arise, they often persist.

Our Desired Self

Finally, there is the desired self. Somewhere among all of our other selves is a self that we believe we could be. This is the self we long for, especially when we are young and planning our future. It is also the source of much discontent in our later life if the desires have not been fulfilled—and they rarely, if ever, are.

Believe the Impossible

The ought-to-be self, desired self, and ideal self share certain commonalities, but they also differ remarkably. There is psychic tension among them and in their totality, substantial tension between them and our so-called actual self.

Now, there's one more thing I wish to add before continuing. What we believe is the actual self is seldom the *true* actual self. The actual self is the result of self-perception and therefore partakes of every believed limitation that accompanies our private self-perception.

If we think back to Nina in the chicken yard, some additional clarity can be added that translates directly to most human eagle/chickens. Within each of us is an almost unlimited possibility—the eagle potential. Within each of us is the sum of all those conflicts, failures, negative message units, and the like—the sum of self-imposed, albeit typically culturally imposed, limitations. Within each of us exists the need to be accepted and also the fear of loss—loss of friends, respect, acceptance, love, and so forth. Within all of us is a cry to soar, in the vernacular of the eagle, and at the same time, a fear of leaving the comfort of our little chicken houses. Within all of us are the secret failures, low or base desires, deeds, and so forth that constitute our perceived actual selves. All of this tension usually holds us almost rigid and stiff, nearly cataleptic, if a change truly threatens any of our four self-images. To add fuel to the fire, change is what most of us truly desire. A true catch-22—damned if we do and damned if we don't.

So how do we safely discover, or uncover, our true potential? What are the limits to our potential—or how high is up?

Innumerable biographies of great people share at least one common denominator—these individuals believed they could do something everyone else, or at least nearly everyone, thought was impossible. These people are the heroes of our world. What made them so convinced they could succeed, despite the crowds that argued to the contrary? That's the next question. If every one of us possessed that conviction and power, would we not all succeed? If the solution was so obvious as to negate choice—that is, if we saw so clearly our direction, ambition, goal, and purpose that there was nothing to choose between—what could stop us from realizing that path?

Let us now look a little deeper into the nature of mind and perception, and then perceptual defense mechanisms—indeed, defense mechanisms in general, but remember and think about this popular notion: *There are three C's in life: Choice, Chance, and Change. You can choose to take a chance and change!*

CHAPTER 5

❀❀❀❀❀

WHAT WE PERCEIVE AND FAIL TO PERCEIVE

"The only way to discover the limits of the possible is to go beyond them, to the impossible."

— ARTHUR C. CLARKE

If choice can be an illusion, what other illusions might we live with? This is such a large subject that we won't even try to take on the question in a comprehensive way. We will, however, look at it sufficiently to clarify for our purposes the most relevant illusions.

Our first illusion is due to language. Language labels everything, and once that is done, that which is labeled is "diminished," in the words of philosopher and theologian Søren Kierkegaard.[1] Nouns are the names of persons, places, and things, yet many nouns refer to things that do not exist. For example, take the noun *griffin.* Arguably, a mythical creature matches this word, but no such creature actually exists. Further, some nouns are really about form, not about things themselves. Take the word *chair.* In the Platonic sense, *chair* refers to a form, that of "chairness." When we attempt to describe a chair, we can be surprised at the definitional ambiguities. Not all chairs have arms or four legs, are stationary, or even are meant to be sat upon, yet somehow when we see a chair, we recognize it as a chair.

Our first illusion is due to language.

Years ago I wrote a piece titled "Sticks and Stones Will Break My Bones but Words Will Slice and Dice Me." The article laid bare a penetrating conclusion: words do more damage to most people in our culture than things do. It's not the words themselves or even Webster's definitions that are damaging or fearsome; rather, the damage is inflicted by the emotive value attached to the words.

It's easy to note the fear of many when they hear words of rejection; words that make fun or are inappropriately critical; words that condemn; and words that negatively label, such as *ugly, stupid, loser,* or *failure.* Words, however, have still other emotional domains that they anchor, or they function like search words in a web browser. When input, they trigger a host of related sites stored deep in our memory. Indeed, due largely to our educational system and culture, most words can be said to have values. Think about it. Even seemingly innocuous descriptors such as color have value attached. Some colors are preferred over others, some colors are simply obnoxious, and for some individuals an emotional disturbance or trauma can be connected to a particular hue.

Knowing and Learning

Our thinking system is such that we have all been taught relative values and judgments. They are reflected in our description of everything we know about ourselves and our surroundings. For most in our culture, words are generally thought to be capable of accurately describing at least the world around us, including ourselves, our feelings, our thoughts, and, of course, our reasons.

Our world is so dependent upon words, semantics, that it's hard to imagine thinking without them. Indeed, thinking seems to presuppose semantic possibilities; after all, how else would we be able to communicate or understand our thinking? Even the images in our dreams are thought to be better understood when we can explain them. So dominant is this thinking priority, this semantic communication necessity, that a failure to be able to communicate linguistically an idea, a feeling, an urge, an intuition, an image, or a sense is thought to be the result of either inadequate education or inadequate basic genetic equipment. After all, where would we be if we couldn't ask such meaningful questions as, *What did that mean to you? How did that make you feel? What do you mean by that? Can you describe the sense, the feeling, the image—or how do you know an intuition is valid and not just fanciful thinking?*

Not only is our world known through semantics—linguistic communication with self and others—but it is modeled by each of us in just this same way. To say that knowing the world through words is quite different from knowing the world through actual sensing participation is obvious and trite. To say that we know ourselves—or better still, model ourselves and our behaviors—through this same word lens should be even more conspicuously ridiculous. Still, for most, it is precisely through the lens of words that both self and the world are known.

We know much more than we know, at least about ourselves. We all came into this world knowing how to naturally sense our environment, how to explore and provide honest feedback about our feelings, how to allow our imaginations to deliver intuitions and images without challenge, and then to feel them for that value alone. But alas, we all learned to be educated and to cherish thinking, not just free thinking, but thinking according to the taught order of correct thinking (e.g., mathematics, logic, and so on). Once the rules of thinking were learned, we were graded on our ability to reproduce the method in our every walk and talk of life, including how we talk to ourselves.

There is a great book titled *A Little Book on the Human Shadow* by Robert Bly that adds yet another relevant dimension here. The idea is simple: not only do we come into the world equipped with honesty and innocence, but we openly express these qualities until we are taught otherwise. At some point others have told us negative things about ourselves—aspects of ourselves that we then begin to hide. Sometimes we tuck these parts away so well that we hide them from ourselves. So when little Johnny is told that it's not okay to get angry, for instance, he hides the anger. When Johnny is told that he shouldn't cry, he hides tear-inducing emotions, and so on.

In Bly's words, he puts it in a "long bag" that he will drag with him all his life.[2] One day the long bag is so full of what we have hidden that we become immobilized by its weight. Growth stops, and we stagnate. Sometimes we are too afraid to look into the long bag, to say nothing of beginning to unload it in healing ways. That does not stop the contents from unloading on us, however. One day Johnny finds himself all tight inside, and suddenly his anger explodes on his wife or children—he is over the top and perhaps without a reason at all.

Subverting Our Natural Selves

As we incorporate our learned methods of thinking with our acquired meanings or values for events and words, we subvert our natural selves to the higher order of being what we should be—unnatural. Our extended dependent maturation made us particularly vulnerable to such basic needs as protection and nourishment and, therefore, additionally vulnerable to supplanting ourselves with the personification of what was expected, what was accepted, what was tolerated, what brought reward, and what avoided punishment. To that extent, even in rebellion, we formed a bond with a self that was perhaps alien to our true selves. Moreover, we anchored all of this emotional memory in and with words, and then we explained ourselves and our emotional outbursts using a socially acceptable vocabulary such as, "It's okay to get even." This only further masked our real feelings (insecurities such as anger, fear, and isolation) while encouraging additional distortions. Of course, there was always the alternative—outright rejection— although this, too, is a distorted perspective. For many people, this distortion translates into a poor self-image: "I'm no good." My research with incarcerated criminals suggests that there is yet another step, or level, to this kind of distortion—the step from high self-alienation to and including high social alienation. When this occurs, the self-image is verbalized more like this: "I'm no good, and neither are you. You [people like you] did it to me. You [someone] made me this way."

As semantic descriptions are built, semantic reactions or responses are encoded and a semantic belief system is coherently hinged to the degree that coherence is possible within the rules of thinking as we have learned them. When incoherence is obvious, a defense mechanism is employed to mask the failure, and semantic distortions are created.

To a cognitive psychologist, this kind of thinking is known as cognitive dissonance, or holding two opposing views, opinions, or beliefs without recognizing that they are mutually exclusive. (Remember the example I used earlier, in which individuals desired to tax the rich until it was their money being taxed.) The outside world, together with the inside world, has at this point become more or less a series of semantic anchors composed of semantic descriptions, semantic reactions, and semantic beliefs and distortions all stitched together like a fisherman's net with semantic references definitionally reinforcing each other.

False to Fact

To use the words of scientist Alfred Korzybski, who developed semantic theory, our world has now become, perhaps more often than any sane person would like to admit, false to fact and therefore necessarily distorted. As Korzybski puts it, the difference between sanity and insanity can be found in false-to-fact distortions that are semantic in nature.[3] It is precisely the mechanism of semantic distortions that underlies thinking processes that are or become neurotic or psychotic, and that gives rise to self-sabotaging behavior and self-limiting beliefs. This very same mechanism—and *mechanism* is a good word because the process becomes so automatic that it operates without our conscious awareness—martials our defenses to action whenever our semantic descriptions, semantic reactions, and semantic beliefs and distortions (semantic processes) are challenged. In fact, the unconscious pervasiveness of the mechanistic nature of these semantic processes is such that even the most knowledgeable of specialists on the matter must maintain a constant vigil to guard against them. This may explain why an individual can succeed brilliantly in a given field and fail miserably in another.

Our language usage, the value and meaning we attach to words, can blind our rational thinking. We could effectively argue that genius escapes this language barrier, for genius goes beyond the boundaries, sees the common differently, and gains a perspective not formerly found. Our world not only assigns values to words but also insists on a sort of "is-ness" property that somehow gives the word an existence of its own. The label, the noun, becomes the thing. The verb may even vicariously become the action.

We all can be fooled by word propositions that address definitional meanings, is-ness, and rules, the so-called logic of our methods and use (or misuse) of language and thinking. A theist could argue that God is all-powerful, while the atheist might refute this claim with such a question as, "Can God create a stone so large he can't lift it?" Word traps and their confusion have led to many atrocities.

It's easy to forget the nature of personal truth when it masquerades in an argument of reason. Logic and linguistics make assertions about many things that are simply false to fact. For example, logic asserts that a gallon is equal to a gallon. This is simply not true from many perspectives, including the most obvious. A gallon of water added to a gallon of alcohol does not equal two gallons of combined fluid. Ergo, $1 + 1 = 2$ is not necessarily so in the "real" world, for no two things are alike in every way. Additionally, it is not possible to know the so-called total of anything. Words are not the things they represent, and what they are supposed to represent is much more, and much less, than could ever be written. Indeed, as has been said many times, probably in its most noteworthy form by the philosopher Ludwig Wittgenstein, "Whatever we say about something, it is also not that." Words are not things, and word things, such as a griffin, do not necessarily exist.

Illusions

So if our words trick us, then that "stream of consciousness," in the words of American philosopher William James, also tricks us. All those inner conversations with ourselves, all the self-talk, trick us just as assuredly. Still, that is not the only illusion our minds are capable of.

> *If our words trick us, then that "stream of consciousness," in the words of William James, also tricks us.*

When in doubt, most people will trust their own judgment and senses—in fact, it is very hard not to trust our own experiences. Yet our biology and psychology function in such a way that we have to question even our own experiences and feelings if we are to have any chance of discovering "the truth." The following illusions are very interesting, and you may be familiar with many of them. The important thing here for you to realize is that if your senses can trick you in this way, what can you really trust? Once you have understood how easily you can be tricked into thinking something that you can see with your own eyes is just not true, then it becomes more conceivable that many other things that you hold to be true may in fact not be so—and your journey to finding yourself can actually begin. A word of caution, though, as William James once said: "A great many people think they are thinking when they are merely rearranging their prejudices."

So, let's start with some visual illusions. We often see what is not there and often fail to see what is. Further, we are very suggestible and can easily see what is suggested. Let's take some common images for purposes of illustration and turn this idea into experience. The following is commonly circulated on the Internet:

Figure 3

Art by Antonio Zamora, derived from a design by A. Kitaoka

Reprinted with permission.

(For links to this and many other illusions that work better in color on a computer screen, go to **www.eldontaylor.com/choicesandillusions**.)

Stare a moment at the image in Figure 3, and you will find that the gears seem to move. Change your gaze from center to corners, and different gears seem to move or move more rapidly. Of course, in reality nothing moves at all.

The next picture should be looked at in a special way. It appears on a page by itself for this reason. When you turn the page, look only at the page. Stare at the center three dots. Concentrate on those dots for one minute. Stare only at the dots, and after that minute, turn and look at a blank wall. Gaze at the wall for approximately 45 seconds. Allow yourself to relax your focus, but keep your gaze on the same space on the wall, even if you think that nothing is going to happen. Something unique will happen, and you should know that this can be done with any number of pictures. What you will see will amaze you, even startle you.

Turn the page, and follow these instructions. Enjoy!

Figure 4

Okay, you just saw a dove soar upward.

The illusion on the next page was chosen to demonstrate how emotions can be tangled with illusions. Everyone knows that a thirsty person in the desert can see a mirage (the illusion of an oasis or simply water) and lose rational abilities in favor of desperate emotions. The next illusion is an emotion-laden illusion. It will evoke a strong emotional response in accordance with a personal belief system. The illusion may please, it may inspire, it may anger—but the point in this context is clear: a simple illusion can evoke strong emotional reactions.

Once again, follow the instructions. Stare this time at the center four dots. Concentrate on those dots for one minute. Stare only at the dots, and after that minute, turn and look at a blank wall. Just gaze at the wall for approximately 45 seconds. Allow yourself to relax your focus, but keep your gaze on the same space on the wall, even if you think nothing is going to happen

Turn the page and follow these instructions.

Figure 5

The next picture illustrates our abilities to see and not to see, or to see differently. This is the rather famous witch and maiden illusion. At first glance, you will see either a witch or a beautiful young maiden. You are typically unable to see both at the same time—at least with conscious recognition. Shift your focus slightly, and the image changes. That is, if you see the witch first, shift your focus and you will see the maiden.

(Please note: these kinds of illusions can be found anywhere and are widely circulated on the Internet.)

Figure 6

Here is another either/or image that is quite famous. It is known as "faces and vases." Can you see both?

Figure 7

The next illusion involves dots. It reminds me of the hidden faces one used to find in the Sunday newspaper. Finding and counting the faces to win something was the purpose of the ad.

Below is a scattering of inkblots. Take a look and notice what you see.

Figure 8

If you look closely, you will see a Dalmatian with its nose down, sniffing the ground. You can make out the dog's ear, nose, shoulder, and left leg first, and the rest fills itself in. Once you see the dog clearly, you cannot help but see it—like the hidden faces in the old Sunday newspapers.

The following image is also a common illusion. Our visual reference system often distorts images according to the background. The shape in the center is really a perfect circle.

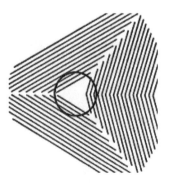

Figure 9

One of my favorite illusions cannot be done on paper. Whether you know it or not, there is a blind spot in the visual field that the brain interpolates (fills in). I encourage you to try this illusion. On my website is a spinning disk (**www.innertalk.com/hypnodisk/hypno.html**). Go to the website or pick up a hypnosis spinning disk and select a picture that you can turn your gaze toward immediately after you focus on the disk. Now stare at the center of the disk as it rotates. Allow your entire consciousness to become totally aware of the spinning disk. Do this for about two minutes. Then turn your gaze toward the picture you previously selected. An amazing thing happens: the still picture suddenly comes alive. It is no longer a two-dimensional image; indeed, it becomes a three-dimensional, moving world.

●◉●

In the provocative film *What the Bleep Do We Know!?*, psychopharmacologist Candace Pert retells a story about the conquistadors and Montezuma. The story, an allegedly factual account, essentially states that when the Spanish galleons approached, they were invisible to the Aztec people. The reason was simply that the Aztec had never seen ships of that nature. When the Spanish approached the shore with their helmets on their heads, what the Aztec perceived were gods with golden helmets reflecting the sun as they walked on water. The Aztec welcomed them as gods, and of course everyone knows what happened. According to the story, it took several days of just staring at the water where the Spanish arrived for one of the Aztec sages to finally see the ships. Arguably, this story illustrates how we fail to see what we see, either because of psychological defense strategies and/or the inability to see what is not already in the mind to see.

A friend of mine, Professor William Guillory, has a model for this nature of perception. It is the so-called reality model and looks like the following diagram.

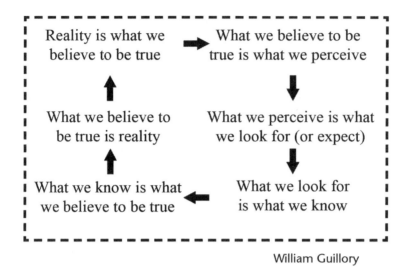

William Guillory

Figure 10

The circularity of our perception becomes obvious after following the arrows in the diagram above. What does not become obvious to many is that the diagram represents reality for most. In other words, most of us can see the circular looping but fail to recognize that it may apply to us.

In the next chapter we will look at defense strategies and once again make some of them an experience. Let me close this chapter with a few more fun illusions.

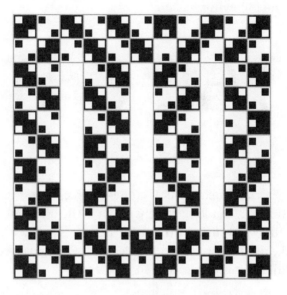

Figure 11

There are no curved lines in the diagram above.

Figure 12

There are only white circles between the black frames.

Read the following:

TAE CAT

Figure 13

This is a classic example of context perception. You probably read, "THE CAT." But look closely. What is the difference between the *H* in the word *the* and the *A* in the word *cat?* Remember, we often make up the context and/or decide on an approved context.

The lines below are really equal in length.

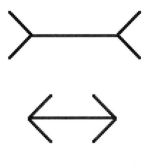

Figure 14

The interesting thing about illusions, as with the previous one, is that even though you know it's an illusion, you nevertheless see the two lines as being of different lengths—the illusion still influences your judgment.

The following photo was used to promote a seminar entitled *Change Without Thinking* that I taught in Malaysia at the Putra Centre.

Figure 15

Did you notice the missing part of the face? Look closely at the space behind the right lens of my glasses. This photo was among a selection of photos I'd had taken. Several months later, after many people had seen and approved the picture for PR purposes, someone noticed the defect behind the glasses. The brain is so used to filling in the blanks that most individuals do not even see a defect such as this until it is pointed out to them.

If this sample of illusions has tricked you, then perhaps taking a closer look at your own expectations, beliefs, perceptions, or perceptual defenses is in order.

Although optical illusions are widely circulated on the Internet, most of the illusions used in this chapter were reprinted with permission from Antonio Zamora at www.scientificpsychic.com. If you enjoy cognitive illusions and would like to see some more, please visit my website, www.eldontaylor.com/choicesandillusions.

CHAPTER 6

◉◈◉◈◉◈◉

Psychological Defense Mechanisms

"Be careful that victories do not carry the seed of future defeats."

— Ralph W. Sockman

A number of psychological defense mechanisms are designed to protect our self-image. Most people are aware of at least some of them. Those that are known as perceptual defense mechanisms include the following:

Denial. As implied by its name, the mechanism of denial is simply one of denying. Often the denial occurs through projection—that is, projecting blame or fault onto another.

Fantasy formation. Fantasy formation creates a perceived reality out of fantasy. If motives cannot be satisfied in the objective external world, they may become a perceived reality in a dream world. Some psychologists suggest that the appeal of much of our entertainment is oriented to satisfying our fantasies for adventure, affection, and security perhaps not so vividly experienced otherwise.

Introjection. Introjection allows one to place blame on oneself. This self-directed blame or punishment defends against disappointment or disillusionment in another. For example, a child feels unworthy of the parent's attention because the parent pays no attention to the child.

Isolation. Isolation involves the avoidance of connecting associations to related ideas that produce anxiety. One set of data is isolated from an associated set: birth is isolated from death, war from mourning, nuclear arsenals from murderous horror, and so forth.

Projection. Projection allows one to project blame or responsibility onto another.

Regression. Regression is a mechanism common during serious illness. Essentially, one regresses to an earlier age, usually as a dependent, when one felt safe and comfortable. The individual returns to an earlier state of development in which someone else assumed responsibility and where fewer, simpler, and more primitive goals existed.

Repression. Generally repression censors or prohibits memories, associations, and adjustments from conscious awareness. Like an invisible filter, this mechanism prevents the conscious mind from "seeing" painful memories and stymied motives. Personal experiences ranging from embarrassment to cruelty are often subject to repression.

Sublimation. Sublimation redirects basic drive mechanisms. Sublimation is simply the substitution of acceptable behavior to satisfy basic motives that might be met equally well in a primitive sense by some form of unacceptable social behavior. Aggression motives, for instance, are often satisfied by sports activities. The process of sublimation is to find avenues in which basic motives may be satisfied in a manner acceptable to the individuals and to society.

In addition to these eight mechanisms, several miscellaneous escapes and defenses are considered by some theorists as contributing to our basic perceptual defenses, which show us only what we want to see about ourselves and the world around us. Several mechanisms can function at one time; in that case, the boundaries overlap, making it difficult to differentiate between the mechanisms.

*Basic perceptual defenses show each of us
only what we want to see about
ourselves and about the world around us.*

Repeated experiments have adequately demonstrated that the conscious mind is not a necessary part of information processing. In fact, the unconscious can, and quite frequently does, operate without the conscious, or is at least unknown to it. Freud once put it this way, "The most complicated achievements of thought are possible without the assistance of consciousness."

Manipulating Your Mind

We're ready now to take a look at an example. Let me first introduce what you are about to see and warn you that some of the images are for adults, not for children. Several years ago an anonymous individual sent me an advertising training manual after reading my book *Subliminal Learning.* The manual described in sophisticated terms the reason for embedding sexual taboos in advertising and provided the graphic example that I will show you. The bottom line to all the psychobabble is this: the sexual embeds are not consciously recognized due to perceptual mechanisms, but the result tends to augment product recognition because of increased dwell time (the time taken to view the ad or even to take a second glance before one turns the page). Judge for yourself.

What follows first is the finished advertisement. Next you will see the artist's rendition made before setting a real model and props in place for a photo session designed to replicate the artist's portrayal. After that you will see the same image, but this time with the embeds outlined so they cannot be missed. Finally, you will see the outlined embeds alone. I have intentionally used four separate pages in this book to prevent visual clues giving away the embeds early. Please take a moment to study the first two pages before viewing the embeds closer. (To see these illustrations in full color, go to **www.eldontaylor.com/choicesandillusions.**)

The advertisement:

Figure 16

The artist's original conceptualization:

Figure 17

A close-up outlining the sexual and taboo embeds:

Figure 18

The outline of the embeds alone:

Figure 19

(Note: this ad was used in 1975. For a link to see it as it appeared back then, and to several other ads that are very similar, please visit **www.eldontaylor.com/choicesandillusions.**)

Once these embeds are pointed out, they are hard to miss, yet they are almost impossible to see when they have not been pointed out. In part this is due to various defense mechanisms—who wants to be accused of having a dirty mind? The most important factor here is that although this information passed beneath your conscious level of perception, it did not get past your subconscious level of perception. Advertisers use subliminals in this way to get you to take a greater interest in their ads, but that is not the focus of our attention now. (For a detailed analysis of this and other ads deploying sexual and demonic images, see my book *Mind Programming*.) Our purpose here is to be aware of just how much information and technology are being used to influence our beliefs, preferences, and choices.

It is also important to know that a number of other mechanisms can conceal information from conscious awareness. Indeed, one of the most interesting to me is how stress, distress, and trauma can virtually hide experience from the conscious mind.

Forensic Hypnosis

For years I practiced criminalistics, and one of my tools was forensic hypnosis. I will never forget receiving a phone call one evening from a local police department. There had been an armed robbery involving a night deposit by a local theater manager. The manager was only able to tell authorities that a "big gun" was pushed into his face just as he was about to pass the money from the driver's side of his vehicle into the night-deposit drawer. The manager surrendered the money and remained still as instructed for several minutes until the thief escaped. Under hypnosis, this same manager was able to tell us in detail about the automobile used by the perpetrators. As it turned out, this manager had formerly been a manager for Hertz and knew automobiles very well. He had seen the car for an instant in his rear-view mirror, as the dome light went on when it pulled in behind him and the gunman jumped from the car while the driver waited for a quick getaway. Under hypnosis, the theater manager provided a complete description of both men, the automobile, and even a partial license plate. The money was recovered, and the suspects were apprehended within a few hours.

Even under the influence of drugs and alcohol, the subconscious remembers. One case I was involved with proved this to me. I was asked to run a lie-detection test and do forensic hypnosis on a young man incarcerated in the state prison for the murder of his mother. He claimed that he confessed to the crime only because of duress and promises of no prison time. He passed the lie-detection test, but that did not necessarily mean anything to me. During hypnosis, however, he was able to provide vivid details regarding his whereabouts at the time of the crime—details that included hiding in the park from police while they searched the trash on an unrelated matter. The time of the homicide, a rather brutal one involving a sex crime as well, made it impossible for this young man to be where he said he was and also to be the perpetrator. The information he had could not have been obtained from any outside source available to him. The police log and other sources confirmed the information, and in a new hearing he was acquitted. On the evening in question, he had been using drugs and alcohol and had no conscious recollection of anything between leaving a party and finding his mother's body, whereupon he phoned law enforcement. Without the aid of hypnosis, he would still be serving time.

•⊙•

Numerous mechanics underlie our perception, or at least our awareness of what we perceive. That is the important point. If all of the information we process, including the so-called no/don'ts we are typically raised with and all of the negative input we receive, both explicit and implied, remains in our subconscious minds, it is no wonder that our thinking and our choices can seem so predisposed. The fact is, we *are* predisposed, and that is the crux of the matter.

Let us now look at your thoughts, how they got there, and whether or not you would choose to think differently.

CHAPTER 7

⊙⊙⊙⊙⊙⊙

WHO OWNS YOUR THOUGHTS ANYWAY?

*"As a single footstep will not make a path on the earth,
so a single thought will not make a pathway in the mind.
To make a deep physical path, we walk again and again.
To make a deep mental path, we must think over and
over the kind of thoughts we wish to dominate our lives."*

— HENRY DAVID THOREAU

As I mentioned earlier, my favorite question to ask these days is, "What was your last truly original thought?" If you listen to my radio show, *Provocative Enlightenment,* or read my books and articles, then you know that I am convinced most people are unable to provide an answer to this question without taking hours to think about it, and some are unable to answer it at all. When you realize that your every ambition, the way you walk, your hand gestures, your clothing, and even your daydreams are built from the ideas of others, then you begin to grasp the issue.

If you question this assertion, take a look at people from different cultures. You will soon find great similarities in expressions, posture, mannerisms, and even handwriting. Once you see this in others, it's a lot easier to look at yourself and find the same thing. This is not to say that it is a cultural issue, but rather to highlight that you too are influenced by everyone around you.

Do you want a particular car because you have been hooked by some sound bite, some photo, some TV commercial? Do you change your behavior when you change your clothes from dressed up to dressed down, since you expect to behave differently when dressed differently? Do you use the information that you consume as the primary mode by which you reason? Is your perception conditioned in such a manner that it forms your expectations, and therefore your perception becomes circular, dependent upon your expectation? In other words, if you expect to see gods walking on water because of a prophecy, as mentioned earlier with the Aztecs, is that what you interpret the conquistador to be? Due to the fact that you have not seen boats of the kind the conquistadors are in or helmets that shine as if made of gold, do you interpret them according to your expectation? Are your interpretations necessary or conditional—necessary in the sense that they occur automatically without critical analysis or conditional based on your evaluating before determining? In what way do you evaluate your perceptions, the beliefs that predispose your perceptions, your thinking, or for that matter your whole stream of consciousness?

Conditioned Perceptions

One of my favorite ways to demonstrate conditioned perceptions is known as the chessboard illusion. As unbelievable as it might sound, we are all so conditioned to see dark/light, dark/light, dark/light on a chessboard, that when two identically colored squares are placed on the board in positions agreeing with our dark/light expectation, we see dark/light despite the fact that they are the same color. That may seem unbelievable, but look at Figure 20. The square marked A and the square marked B are actually the same color! When I first showed this to my wife, she could not, or would not, believe it. However, you can test this out for yourself by making a couple of photocopies of Figure 20 and cutting the A and B squares out of one of the copies. Place these two squares on the white part of the page and you will see they are the same. Slide them onto the board to their respective positions, and all of a sudden they will appear different. Now, if you play around with the cutouts and move them to different positions on the board, it may seem as if this dark/light/dark concept does not always hold constant. It is true that the shadow effect does play a role in how you perceive the colors on this board, but all of this only goes to prove quite how easily your perceptions can be manipulated. If you can be deceived this easily, simply by using the chess board and a slight shadow, what other subtle techniques are being used to influence you?

Figure 20

(Reprinted courtesy of Professor Edward H. Adelson, John and Dorothy Wilson Professor of Vision Science, Department of Brain and Cognitive Sciences, MIT. Website: **http://persci.mit.edu/people/adelson**.)

The Investment in Our Minds

It would amaze and horrify you to know the extent to which others engineer our thoughts. Billions and billions of dollars have been spent by governments and marketing researchers to determine exactly how our minds work, especially our unconscious or subconscious (I use those two terms in this instance as synonyms). What have they learned? Here are just a few of the discoveries made by those in the field of what today is known as *scientific marketing*.

Using fMRI to view the brain functioning in real time, it has been demonstrated that showing a smoker the surgeon general's warning on a pack of cigarettes excites a reward center in the brain that motivates them to smoke more. Message: put the warning on more sides of the pack and make it bold.

It has been shown that subliminally flashing a smiling face on a foreign flag predisposes one to feel more favorably about the country the flag represents.[1] Marketers know that if a beautiful woman is draped over an automobile hood, men will judge that automobile to be faster than others. Researchers have found that incorporating death and dying themes into advertisements excites the Thanatos urge and leads to arousal. (The Thanatos urge is a Freudian concept, also known as the death instinct, and some activities are seen as death defying and therefore very exciting and inviting.) They know that sexual embeds that are placed in advertisements are not consciously perceived, but they nevertheless cause arousal, which is most often interpreted as positive. In one study, it was found that when men crossing a dangerous bridge are met by a young woman, they are much more likely to phone her in an attempt to hook up than men who encounter this same woman on a park bench.[2] I could go on in much greater detail, but that is not the purpose of this book. (If you would like to learn more, please read *Mind Programming*.) My point here is not the many things known about us that we might deny, but that they are known and used daily. The result is, *What was your last original thought?*

Whose Thoughts Are You Thinking?

As I've already noted, our unconscious mind is actually making our decisions—at least most of them! How does it do this? The information we have input throughout our life—all of it, whether from parents, peers, games, television, or any other form of communication, including billboards, print and electronic media, and the like—is what's in the unconscious. Add to that our experiences, good and bad, and the defense mechanisms that have been built up to protect us, our method of reasoning, our long bags, and so forth—and while adding, remember to allow in your calculations for the fact that humans are herd animals and by nature seek acceptance and operate primarily on the principle of pleasure over pain. Now you are ready to at least approximate the calculus deployed in your unconscious mind for decision making.

Suffice it to say, in our modern technological age we are more a product of nurture, at least in the sense of our total enculturation, than of nature. Interestingly, when someone comes along to point that out to you, they are typically ridiculed, criticized, and otherwise attacked in order to have their observations invalidated. One of the most effective tools can be summed up by H. L. Mencken's words: "A good belly laugh is worth a thousand syllogisms." Instead of meeting argument with argument, logic with logic, dismiss it by making some joke that in itself degrades the message or the messenger. Think of it this way: Sarah Palin never said she could see Russia from her kitchen, but the joke stuck, and many people today still believe that those were her words when discussing her experience in matters of national security. Here's another example—if you present information that suggests a possible conspiracy, you're likely to get a comment in return about your tinfoil hat.

The fact is, as much as we all hate to admit it, *they* already own our thoughts! I am currently working on a new book (tentatively entitled *Gotcha* and due out in 2014) that will provide all the proof that the most skeptical of skeptics would ever need about how psychological discoveries are being used in real-world scenarios. For now, however, let me provide just a few examples. Dan Ariely, professor of psychology and behavioral economics at Duke University, has shown that when we don't know something about a person, most of us are likely to fill in that blank in a positive way. Is it just coincidence that we know less about President Barack Obama than any other United States President in history, and that his people ignore claims that we know little?

Are you aware of the team of psychologists President Obama used during his campaigns? Quoted in the *New York Times* article, Craig Fox, a member of this team, refers to the group of professionals as a "kind of dream team" of behavioral scientists.[3] They consisted of Fox, professor of psychology at the University of California,

Los Angeles; Susan T. Fiske, professor of psychology at Princeton University; Samuel L. Popkin, professor of political science at the University of California, San Diego; Robert Cialdini, regents' professor of psychology and marketing at Arizona State University; Richard H. Thaler, professor of behavioral science and economics at the University of Chicago's graduate school of business; and Michael W. Morris, professor of leadership at Columbia University. The team provided information not just from existing research, but guidance as to the "little things that can make a difference." The *Times* article said: "At least some of the consortium's proposals seemed to have found their way into daily operations. Campaign volunteers who knocked on doors last week in swing states like Pennsylvania, Ohio and Nevada did not merely remind people to vote and arrange for rides to the polls. Rather, they worked from a script, using subtle motivational techniques that research has shown can prompt people to take action."[4]

Gotcha

Bottom line, it is big business to own your every thought. When you think hungry, think fast food; when you're thirsty, think soda pop; when you're anxious—well, you get the picture. Whether it is politicians or pitch artists, the point is to get you to think what they want you to think, and if they are really good at their job, you will also deny categorically that your thoughts have been manipulated—at least with regard to their particular subject. All of this means that the more passionate you are about a subject, the more you need to examine your thoughts again.

Today we are a consumption society that largely uses shopping to assuage anxiety. In doing so, we create more anxiety, but it is in the future and doesn't arrive until we begin to experience the money crunch. The credit-card bills roll in, and the anxiety builds . . . so we go shopping again. Make sense? If not—why do so many people continue to follow this pattern? Do you?

This chapter has been a brief introduction to the idea that our thoughts may be owned less by us than they are by others. Deciding to engineer our own, to carefully select and choose the information that we put in our minds, is entirely up to each of us as individuals.

If you choose to continue to take in every advertisement and sound bite without questioning, without discernment, then you can expect no more than a result based on others' desires. It is your choice, and this one is not an illusion unless you choose not to make it. Think on that.

⊙

Now that I have shown you how your thoughts may have been manipulated, let us take a look at one of my favorite subjects—subliminal communication, or, as I prefer to call it, information processing without awareness. In the following chapter, I will attempt to separate the fact from the fiction and expose the so-called controversy. In doing so, we will look at the varying definitions and the most current research findings.

Much of the information you have processed in your lifetime has been information that has passed beneath your conscious sentry, or recognition.

Information processing without awareness becomes particularly relevant to our purpose for two reasons. First, much of the information you have processed in your lifetime has been information that passed beneath your conscious sentry, or recognition. Second, it is potentially a very useful tool for changing self-talk, and thereby affecting expectation, self-limiting beliefs, and so forth. As such, once you have a good grasp of this subject, you will discover how you can turn the tables on the mind manipulators and actually take back control of your own thoughts.

CHAPTER 8

⊙◈◈◈⊙

INFORMATION PROCESSING WITHOUT AWARENESS

"A certain amount of opposition is a great help to a man. Kites rise against, not with, the wind."

— JOHN NEAL

In the early 1980s I heard that the Los Angeles Police Department had experimented with subliminal programs for a terrorist-abduction scenario as part of their preparation for the Summer Olympics the city hosted in 1984. The idea was a simple one. Because so much time is typically spent in negotiations over the phone, the subliminal messages would suggest illness. These messages were designed to produce physiological responses similar to what would be expected if you had been exposed to a viral agent that led to diarrhea, vomiting, and malaise. The masking sound was supposedly that of a furnace, or what is known as pink noise. I was told that the police department tested this program and then suspended it after three days because it was dehydrating cadets. I have never been able to find either confirmation or denial for this report, so I don't honestly know if it was done or not. What I do know is that the story piqued my interest in subliminal communication.

My initial exploration into information processing without awareness had nothing to do with using it as a countermeasure for mind programming, because my business at the time was criminalistics. I owned an agency that, among other things, ran several hundred lie-detection tests a year. One of the problems encountered in deception testing is known as "inconclusives." That is, the charts are not clear enough to say with confidence that deception is indicated or that the test is nondeceptive. Inconclusives can be the product of poor test structure and preinterview techniques or, more commonly, countermeasures or situational stress. The gist of it is that honest people are so nervous about the test results that their anxiety spills across all questions in such a way as to lower the net differential between relevant questions and prestressed, control, or irrelevant questions. Dishonest people employ some countermeasure, such as the proverbial tack in the shoe, and selectively administer discomfort to themselves during irrelevant questions, again possibly skewing the differential. I simply thought how wonderful it would be to use a subliminal program to ease the situational stress for the honest and to heighten it for those who intend to deceive.

The Subliminal Controversy

To make a long story short, I decided to find out more about subliminal communication. The literature even then was rather robust with research demonstrating the efficacy of subliminal communication. Unfortunately for me, most of the work employed visual subliminal methods, such as the tachistoscope (a device that displays an image for a specified amount of time, as in 1/100th of a second), and this simply would not work in my intended application. The remaining literature dealt with audio but under tightly controlled conditions, in which hearing tests for individual thresholds of conscious perception were conducted first and the ambient background noise was controlled so as not to add noise to signal-strength ratios. I found, however, a number of anecdotal reports that ranged from curbing shoplifting to eliminating fainting while waiting for medical procedures. Most of the anecdotal evidence I came across had something to do with the Becker Black Box (a device designed to insert subliminal audio messages in a public music system, such as the kind you would find in a retail store).

As with many others, my early knowledge regarding sublimi-nal technology arose from the popular media. There were the now infamous cola and popcorn stories about James Vicary, who claimed to increase concession sales by flashing such things as "hungry—eat popcorn" on Kim Novak's face during the showing of the movie *Picnic*. Contrary to popular opinion, this may have never happened. Vicary had intended to sell a subliminal projector to theaters around the country, but when he was asked to testify before Congress regarding the alleged popcorn messages, he denied making them. We do know, however, that he had the capability. The Congressional hearings in 1984 regarding subliminal com-munication and the outrage of the American public, the entire Orwellian fear mentality of the time, may have induced him to deny doing such a thing. (For more information, see my book *Mind Programming*.)

Protection Against Subliminal Influence

Books by Norman Cousins and Vance Packard shouted out fear messages regarding the power of subliminal communication. Cousins termed this technology potentially the most dangerous ever developed. Packard, in *The Hidden Persuaders,* spoke of how it could be used to manipulate the public. Then along came Wilson Brian Keyes, whose books pictorially illustrated the use of sublimi-nal messages in everything from menus to Playboy advertisements. The alarmed public demanded something be done to protect them from this invasion of their minds. There were hearings and articles, but in the end no laws were passed to prevent the use of mind pro-gramming.[1] In the United States, the FCC did create a codification that is supposed to prevent the broadcast of subliminal messages. The unfortunate truth of the matter is that more than one case has been taken to the FCC and no penalties have ever been imposed. Even the now infamous "RATS" ad that appeared on television dur-ing the Bush/Gore presidential campaign failed to move the FCC to do anything more than condemn. You may recall that in this advertisement, the subliminal message bolded above Mr. Gore's head was "RATS," taken from the small print BureaucRATS. The Democrats cried foul, and the people behind the Bush advertisement first asserted "accident" and then conceded intention, but that it was just a joke and not meant to be taken seriously.

You might be interested to know that researchers at Adelphi University conducted an experiment replicating the Bush/Gore campaign and the infamous "RATS" ad and found that the ad definitely skewed the election in favor of the Bush-like candidate. They therefore concluded that it was very likely that the ad did influence the outcome of the election. That said, despite the Democratic Party pursuing this as far as it could, nothing happened—there was nothing they could do. That tells all of us that if they could do nothing, no one can do anything about this sort of subliminal influence.

Another point worth noting regarding the law has to do with legislation proposed in the state of Utah. This legislation would not have made the use of subliminal information illegal; it would simply have required informed consent. So, if a retailer wished to use subliminal antitheft messages, that would be fine—provided the retailer published the fact that such messages were used and made the affirmations available upon request. The reason for the latter was simply due to some so-called antitheft messages I had seen. Bear in mind that a message such as "Buying is honest" is also a motivational message, not just one discouraging theft. The legislation was approved by the committee after a veritable who's who in the advertising world showed up in Utah to oppose it. The opposition loudly asserted that the law was unnecessary since no one used subliminal messages, and that they would not do so simply because they did not work in the first place. Although the committee approved the proposed law, it never went to the floor for a vote.

To this day, no legislation protects
the consumer from subliminal manipulation.

A representative of a foreign politician contacted my office regarding subliminal advertising. I advised against using it unless it was done with full disclosure. For example, informing the public that you were using a subliminal message to get out the vote might attract favorable attention to both the politician and the campaign.

On the other hand, it could backfire. Either way, if it was used it would in all probability be discovered.

The Secret Recipe

Now back to my story. Because many companies were offering subliminal tapes, I phoned a number of them. I explained who I was and asked how they made their tapes. You would have thought I was asking for the secret recipe for Coca-Cola. In my opinion, companies that made so-called scientific claims were obligated to provide at least some information regarding how they prepared a program that supposedly altered behavior. No one was forthcoming. Eventually I purchased some programs and sent them to Audio Forensic Laboratories in California for analysis. When I received the report, I knew why the matter was such a secret. The bottom line was that there were no subliminal messages on the tapes—on any of them. At least, there was no recoverable verbal content of any kind.

It was clear that for a stimulus to affect someone, there must be sufficient signal strength. Subtract the signal strength, and everything became about as subliminal as something being said a mile away. For some this result may have been satisfactory because, after all, the mind was magical and it could extract verbal messages from the ether. This notion did not work for me, however, so I went back to the drawing board.

Dichotic Listening

Reviewing the literature again, I found quite a bit of good audio work on what is called shadowing, or dichotic listening, experiments. Essentially, this type of work masks one message with another. One ear may receive random numbers for a period while the other perceives a partial story, then the partial story switches to the numbers ear and the numbers switch to the story ear. Subjects normally report hearing the story and fail to report the numbers. Sometimes random words are presented to one ear and a partial story to the other. The brain selects the words it needs to complete, or fill in, the story, which is simultaneously delivered to the opposite ear. See the following illustration.

Figure 21

In a typical shadowing task, the messages are presented simultaneously to the left and right ears, and the subject attempts to shadow one ear.

Figure 22

Here the subject follows the meaningful message as it moves from one ear to the other.

Mirror Image

Now I must take a step or two backward. I was familiar with something called "back masking," and a sound engineer for a couple of major artists had told me that he personally mixed backward messages into their songs. I was also convinced that children mixing up 5's and S's by writing them backward, as so very many seem to do, were simply correcting for some mirrored image in the mind. Further, the holographic models put forth by such researchers as Karl Pribram and David Bohm had provided a simple mechanic by which this speech reversal, or mirroring, was accomplished. I have referred to this mirroring model as the MIP method, or Mirror Imaging Paradigm, in my books on subliminal information. As you may recall, Karl Pribram, the noted neuroscientist, and David Bohm, the Nobel Prize–winning physicist, advanced the theory that the brain stores information holographically—that is, across all of the brain. According to this theory, every cell carries information, or, more specifically, memories, like a tiny piece of holographic film. (When a film plate catches a holographic image, the plate can be cut into many pieces; but when light shines through any of the pieces, the contents of the entire plate are visible. In other words, unlike a picture cut into several pieces, perhaps forming a puzzle, every fragment of the holographic film contains the entire image.)

*The right hemisphere is the spatial, creative,
and nonlinear hemisphere; the left hemisphere is
subject to the rules of language, logic, and linear thinking.*

Brain hemispheric specialization theories argue that the right hemisphere, for typical right-handed people, is the spatial, creative, and nonlinear hemisphere; whereas the left hemisphere is subject to the rules of language, logic, and linear thinking. The right hemisphere is also the seat of the unconscious or subconscious. Using simple deductive reasoning, it occurred to me that the right hemisphere probably acquired language first, because its development by way of specialization precedes the left. (Infants first perceive dark and light, then shapes, and so forth.) If this were the case, and since hard research has proven that memory is indeed stored across all of the brain,[2] then word representations in an oversimplified model may look like the following illustration.

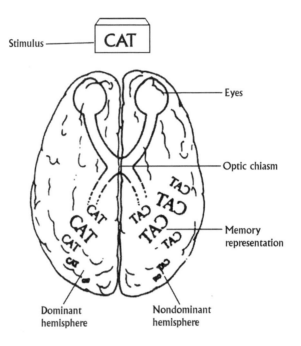

Figure 23

Reverse Speech

I added this all up, and the light dawned. What if I were to mask forward speech with reverse speech? Would this confuse the mind enough for it to fail to consciously discriminate the speech? You see, hemispheric specialization explained the famous Stroop Effect, in my view. Because one hemisphere entertained more than the other such things as space and color while the other hemisphere dealt with the rules of language, logic, and so forth, when a person is called upon to integrate the two, there is a noticeable failure. The Stroop Test prints the names of various colors in colors that to do not correspond with the name of the color. For example, the word *yellow* would be printed in green, the word *blue* printed in red, and so forth. (If you would like to try this test for yourself, please go to **www.eldontaylor.com/choicesandillusions**.)

What most people find is that there is substantial interference between the spelling of the word and the color of the typeface. What should be a simple task becomes quite difficult. Combining this information, I decided to deliver both forward speech and reverse speech and disguise it with a soundtrack—sounds of the ocean with birds or music. In doing so, I found that a person's ability to discriminate the speech was almost entirely lost. In time, this became known as the Taylor Method, and I patented it, together with some other claims, totaling 105 in all. (This technology is known as InnerTalk today.) When I ran studies, at least everyone would be able to see exactly how we did things by simply viewing the patent and, as with all good science, test or replicate my findings.

All right, I had a method. And, by the way, unknown to me at the time, another researcher by the name of David Oates was simultaneously working on reverse speech. There is little doubt today that some children process language in reverse. (You might want to visit his website, **www.reversespeech.com**, and listen for yourself.) We often mistake as gibberish the speech of small children in the phase of development where the child looks you right in the eye and says something that is not goo-goo gaga, but you don't understand what he or she is saying. Yet, when such speech is played backward, it is meaningful, such as "Daddy, help!"

What is more, various law-enforcement agencies have learned, as I did, that reversing the answers in a statement may reveal some interesting information. This first happened to me when I was manually reversing a reel-to-reel tape recording made at 7 inches per second (IPS) to replay it at 15/16 IPS through a Psychological Stress Evaluator, a method of truth verification. As I manually turned the spool on my Uher recorder, the forward answer "no" became "liar." This astounded me, especially when the charts agreed that deception was present. A confession taken later verified that the subject was indeed lying. How was this possible? Well, the exact mechanics are not known. What has been verified, though, is that reverse speech can add information, refute statements, and often do even more. In one criminal case, for example, statements that dealt with an armed robbery actually revealed the location of the hidden money when they were slowed down and played in reverse. As with the so-called Freudian slip, apparently the subconscious needs to get in its proverbial two bits' worth as well.

Choosing the Messages

My new method gave rise to the detection of occasional speech sounds, such as someone talking softly, but the words were not consciously discriminated. The next problem I had to solve was with regards to the messages I should use on my program. What message would give rise to minimizing distress in a detection of deception examination unless the subject intended to practice deception—and then have the reverse effect? This was not easy, but in the end I elected to use two components: the statement "The truth shall set you free" and the entire 23rd Psalm. (The 23rd Psalm was used by many prisoners of war during WWII and the Korean War, according to their reports, to assuage the anxiety and stress of capture.) The results astonished me. Not only did inconclusives disappear, but confession rates soared. In fact, there were times I thought of saying, "Stop, don't tell me yet—I get paid by the hour."

The Prison Study

I reported my findings to some of the local law-enforcement agencies and heard back that the prosecutor did not think our using this technology was such a good idea, so we stopped. Still, now that I knew this could work in a lie-detection scenario, I wondered about using it to rehabilitate prison inmates. A friend of mine from the Utah State Prison staff, Lee Liston, approached me with the initial idea, and we went to work on setting up a rather extensive study. We called upon another friend, Dr. Charles McCusker, a psychometric specialist, and set up a study using the Minnesota Multiphasic

Personality Inventory (MMPI), which is the clinical instrument most often used to provide an objective measure of personality. It is employed quite often in court cases and is generally deemed the most reliable instrument for personality assessment.

Our study used prison inmates who volunteered to take part. They were divided into three groups: an experimental group that would receive the messages designed to lower hostility and aggression and improve chances at rehabilitation (interrupt the recidivism rate), a placebo group that would listen to the sounds of the ocean without messages, and a control group that would do nothing. The study was to take place over 30 days, with the inmate volunteers listening to the programs a minimum of one hour a day every day.

The MMPI was administered using a modified version developed for the incarcerated environment, known as the Fowler Lens. The MMPI was used first to determine a so-called common denominator. The results yielded no real surprises, as there were high scores in both social and self-alienation. We decided to use the Thurstone Temperament Schedule (a psychometric instrument/questionnaire/scale designed to measure behavior) before and after the test to determine what effect our InnerTalk program had. However, I was still faced with the question, "What do we say to the inmates?"

It's okay to do better than Daddy.
Mommy and I are one.

The research literature had only two magic messages. The work of Dr. Lloyd H. Silverman, a research psychologist at the Veterans Administration in New York, demonstrated that the message "It's okay to do better than Daddy" had remarkable results in a variety of domains, and the "Mommy and I are one" message seemed to have universal power, from improving dart-throwing ability to reducing symptoms of schizophrenia. Silverman theorized that Freudian complexes were often sublimated in adaptive ways that could lead to schisms in the psyche, which led him to the subliminal message, "Mommy and I are one."[3] My own work (as I have set out in my other books) suggests that this "Mommy" is not our actual physical mother, but rather the universal archetype of motherhood, namely the womb. The womb—whether of a mother or of nature, the planet, or the living consciousness known as Gaia—is a place of sanctuary. Indeed, Silverman's own work showed that the message had no effect if the subject was conscious of its presence. *How wonderful,* I thought in reviewing this literature. *However, I somehow don't think that the "Mommy" message is quite enough with our prison population.* So what message or messages should be used on the program?

> *Researchers at Boston University's Center for Brain*
> *and Memory have pinpointed the mechanism*
> *that makes subliminal learning work.*

It was time to speak with the inmates and let them tell us what should be on the program. What we discovered changed my life and could change yours. In the next chapter, we will review this information, and I will again attempt to make it personal with some stories and experiential material. In chapters to come, I will share other experiences and offer my opinions on what is behind some of the misconceptions regarding subliminal communication. It is worth noting that today there is little controversy. Even the neurological mechanism for subliminal learning has been identified. In May 2005, a team of researchers, led by Takeo Watanabe of Boston University's Center for Brain and Memory, announced that his team had "pinpointed the mechanism that makes subliminal learning work."[4]

◉◉◉◉◉

CHAPTER 9

A SIMPLE MODEL OF MIND AND BEHAVIOR

"You have powers you never dreamed of. You can do things you never thought you could. There are no limitations in what you can do except the limitations of your own mind."

— DARWIN P. KINGSLEY

When I have spoken to inmates, they all have stories and persons or events on which to blame their life errors. In lectures, I have often summed up their attitudes this way: "Ah, but for the grace of God, you would be where I am today. My mother was a prostitute, and my daddy an alcoholic. The neighbor boy hung heroin on me when I was 12." Et cetera, et cetera, et cetera. In other words, their situation is not their fault. Even when their stories are false or greatly exaggerated, it still is not their fault. They all have someone or something to blame. They would seek to gain understanding and even sympathy with their life stories. Not that some of the stories are not touching, but my point is that the function of blame essentially removed their responsibility through rationalizations such as "What would you have done?" or "Maybe it was wrong, but what else could I do?" Their choices are framed in experience much like those in our flowerpot story.

The inmates generally have a compensation mechanism that differs from that of people in society. Remember the high scores in social and self-alienation. Typically, the person with low self-esteem tends to adapt by thinking of others as better. This was not necessarily true in our inmate population. Many of them had compensated this way: "If I'm no good, you're no good. Do unto others before they do unto you. Don't get even; get 'evener.'"

The Magic Bullet

For the record, I have discovered that what I am about to share with you works everywhere. It worked in the prison system, and it works in hospice centers. It works with elite professional athletes, Fortune 500 types, small children, and everyone in between. It works in Germany, China, Malaysia, Singapore, Mexico, Canada, India, England, Ireland, and more. I know it works there because we have distributors and customers, as well as studies, coming from these areas. I am convinced that it works everywhere, in every language, and on all human beings.

What, then, to put on the prison subliminal program? It should be obvious, but allow me to digress for a moment. There are two ways to be tied up in the world. In one way, another person binds you. In the other way, you choose to hold on to a tiny thread attached to anything and refuse either to let go or pull hard enough to break it. You might feel as if you're walking around, but as soon as you reach the thread's end, you turn and retreat. It's interesting that this is how elephants are trained. Tying elephants when they are very young with large chains causes them to soon learn that they are attached, and if they try to run the ground will suddenly be jerked out from under them and they will fall and hurt themselves. When these animals are fully grown and could easily snap the chain, they are content tied only with a small rope. They choose—if you can use that word in this context—not to test the boundary.

Similarly, blame is a bind—pure and simple, it ties you up!

As long as we blame, we effectively rob ourselves of our own empowerment. After all, if it's not my fault, then there is nothing I can do about it. The "everything sucks and then you die" attitude, the "it's not my fault" approach, and similar beliefs strip individuals of the power to affect their own world. The net result, as R. D. Laing so eloquently says in *Politics of Experience,* is:

> The condition of alienation, of being asleep, of being unconscious, of being out of one's mind, is the condition of the normal man.
>
> Society highly values its normal man. It educates children to lose themselves and to become absurd, and thus to be normal.
>
> Normal men have killed perhaps 100,000,000 of their fellow normal men in the last fifty years. . . .
>
> We are not able even to think adequately about the behavior that is at the annihilating edge. But what we think is less than what we know; what we know is less than what we love; what we love is so much less than what there is. And to that precise extent we are so much less than what we are.

As long as we blame, we effectively rob ourselves of our own empowerment.

Now, let us build a model and see if we can find the gears and tumblers that cause all of this nonsense to seem sensical. In Figure 24, the circle represents the mind.

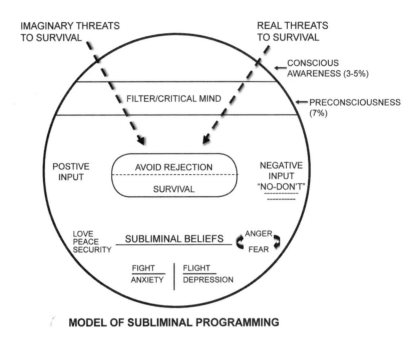

MODEL OF SUBLIMINAL PROGRAMMING

Figure 24

According to the notion that we use 10 percent or less of our brain/mind, our model shows that 3 percent is conscious awareness at any given time; 7 percent or so is preconscious, or that part of our mind that accesses, say, the verse to a favorite song that we do not carry around full-time in our conscious mind; and the remaining 90 percent is untapped resources and our subconscious or unconscious. Here I am again using *subconscious* and *unconscious* synonymously, despite my being fully aware that there is a sharp demarcation between the two in psychological literature.

Stimuli

At the bottom of the diagram you find fight/flight over anxiety/depression. In modern man, fight has become anxiety (preparedness to fight, a heightened state of arousal) and depression has replaced flight. In fact, in cases of chronic depression, the subjects have fled inward so much that they often withdraw almost completely from the outer world.

Notice that above the circle are indicated two forms of stimuli. Real stimuli might be that old saber-toothed tiger or a .357 Magnum held to our head. Now, why the synthetic stimuli? Synthetic here refers to something that is not life threatening, as with a real stimulus, but to which we respond as though it were. In other words, when our bodies go to the budget we identified earlier as defense, the old anxiety and/or depression kick in. Whether the stimulus is real or imagined (synthetic), our bodies respond chemically. For many individuals that synthetic stimulus can be a look from their employer, a word from their significant other, a letter in the mail making some demand, or even someone cutting in front of them and "flipping them off" during rush-hour traffic. Because the synthetic stimuli are what most of us live with, it is fair to ask: What makes these stimuli capable of triggering a fight/flight, anxiety/depression response?

Let us look again at our model. We see rejection avoidance over survival. It would appear that our need to be accepted, respected, and so forth is weighted as equal or nearly equal to our drive to survive. A basic human need is acceptance. Whether this is to accommodate the so-called basic drives covered earlier or for some other reason is not so clear—but the fact is, we do all need to be accepted and loved. Something intrinsic is threatened when we are cut off in traffic or met with disdain and rejection from another human being, particularly one who has power of some kind over us.

What is also interesting about this synthetic stimulus is that it is not the same for all of us. A stressful stimulus to some is a sought-after stimulus for others. One factor is universal, and that follows in a construct model of the mind. Look again at our model. Beneath the rejection/survival is something I have labeled "subliminal beliefs." Our subconscious beliefs, some of which we know and some we do not, create a sort of calculus. Imagine a measuring stick with -10 on one end and +10 on the other. At one end would be -10 units of pleasure (which becomes 10 units of pain), and at the other end, 10 units of pleasure. Jeremy Bentham called this a "hedonic calculus."[1] Using this measurement, we can scale belief from a point of love/peace/security to anger/fear. On opposite ends of the line in our model representing these unconscious, or subliminal, beliefs, we find a scale that can be thought of this way. Most human beings seek to feel loved and secure, and much behavior is built around avoiding rejection. When our beliefs are threatened, the result moves the scale toward anger and fear.

In the typical parenting/peer-related maturation process, each of us receives a quantity of input. Some of it is positive, but much is negative. All the no/don'ts and self-limiting beliefs are posited here in our subliminal beliefs. Every time we have been told we are stupid, unattractive, fat or skinny, not old enough, not smart enough, and so forth, it has been recorded in our subconscious mind. These no/don'ts combined with the "shoulds" and "oughts" form the mold for our beliefs. Among them are those trainings that have been acquired from our entertainment, like the right to get even. All of this nonsense becomes what we believe—our reality, which anchors our self-definition and experience and serves as a loop to reinforce our beliefs. Our language, experience, and feedback have been programmed without our conscious awareness or agreement.

Years ago I created a couple of acronyms for anger and fear. They are circular. Anger = *A* Nasty *G*etting *E*ven *R*esponse. Fear = *F*or *E*very *A*nger *R*esponse. So for every anger response, there is a nasty getting-even response. There is no such thing as anger without fear. Some of the so-called tough guys in the world should get this—there is no such thing as anger without a fear attached!

> *For Every Anger Response*
> *there is*
> *A Nasty Getting Even Response.*

What is the fear, you might ask? The fear can be any number of things. It can vary from "you took something from me," including my space in the queue during rush-hour traffic (acceptance/respect), to "you don't believe the same way I do," which again is oriented toward avoidance of rejection.

Blame

What I discovered with the prison inmates was the ability to displace responsibility. A function not shown in our model is known as blame. This is the way we escape responsibility, and it too is defined by our culture. To justify irrational behavior, thoughts, and so forth, even if we fail to recognize the irrational nature of it all, we blame. The inmates blamed. It was not their fault, and we should understand that. The actual facts might be quite different—not that some negativity wasn't present—but many people face the same obstacles and make entirely different choices from criminality.

I like to think of obstacles as opportunities. Why not, after all? It is much more pragmatic to deal with challenges in a positive manner than in a negative one, if for no other reason than health and personal well-being—the old body chemicals, remember? Indeed, let me share a real pragmatic viewpoint with you. I have learned to approach life with an attitude of gratitude. Long before that became a popular idea, and largely from my own research and work such as that with the inmate prison population, I discovered that an antidote to negativity could be had by just changing the way I defined certain things. So, when someone makes a comment or something happens that might produce stress, anger, and so forth, I invoke this little phrase:

"I can't wait to see what good happens from this."

I choose to look at the world as providing everything I need right now. I choose to think that everything that comes to me does so for some good. Finding that good might not always be so easy, but thinking this way transforms the poison that might otherwise accumulate in my body, such as cortisol. Cortisol is a chemical stored in the body as a result of stress. Anger and fear, blame and shame are stressors that generate this chemical. Cortisol kills, literally. It has been linked to early aging and various diseases, as well as brain degeneration. It is not something any rational person really wants to create, let alone save.

So with my new attitude, I pulled into my office parking lot one bright summer morning. As I passed a video store in the same strip mall, a driver suddenly backed from his parking stall into the side of my new car. Smash! My first thought was not my preferred one, but I quickly adjusted and rather snidely said aloud to myself, "I can't wait to see what good happens from this!"

The driver of the car that slammed into me jumped from his vehicle, yelling obscenities. He claimed that I had hidden behind his old beat-up jalopy just so he would hit me. *Right,* I thought. *I hid my new Cadillac behind your junk heap just so you could hit me.* I only smiled at the older man and his cussing. As it happened, law-enforcement officers were in the parking lot and saw the entire incident. They too got an earful of how I had hidden behind the jalopy just so I could get hit. It was sad—except that it was funny. This older gentleman had no insurance or driver's license. That didn't matter to me, because my insurance policy covered uninsured motorists. Well, the long and the short of it is my car was fixed as good as new, my body chemicals were those of laughter, although I did not laugh at the man, and his body chemicals—well, you get the picture. The pure pragmatist in me saved who knows how much cortisol from my system and, as with the flowerpot, what good would getting mad have done anyway?

Undoing the Blame Game

Back to our prison inmates. Their mechanism, blame, essentially displaced their personal responsibility. Further, unlike most people, their self-esteem social issues gave rise to a philosophy that can be stated this way: "If I'm no good, then you aren't either." This is an inverted form of the "I'm okay, you're okay" idea. As such, a sort of "Do unto others before they do unto you" credo existed, even if they did not overtly recognize it.

Here was our clue—now we could plan what to say on our subliminal program. We had to undo the blame game. As I mentioned earlier, there are essentially two ways to be tied up in the world.

Someone can physically bind you or you can hold on to some thread and refuse to pull it hard enough to break it, and you are just as tethered as if you were actually tied. Holding on to blame is the same as being tied up. Until it is released, there is nothing you can do about anything, because, after all, it's not your fault. If it is not your fault, then how can anyone, including you, expect you to take responsibility for the issue? If you are not responsible, then you are not empowered to make changes. In other words, the blame game disempowers—directly. Indeed, to the precise extent we blame anything or anyone, we surrender our empowerment franchise.

Bad-luck fortune-cookie collectors.

Interestingly, however, there are those who cling to their "right" to blame. I have a friend in South Africa who is a lie-detection examiner. He has a model I like. He calls it something else, but we'll call it the "bad-luck fortune cookies" game. So, this is the story of these special cookie collectors. They go through life collecting all the cookies they can. Riding on the escalator of life, they will even jump high in the air to catch one, just so they can put it in their backpack of life experience and share it later. And share they do. Each evening, whether at home or in the pub, on the telephone or via e-mail, they tell their friends all about the cookies of the day. These sharings go like this:

> *First Person:* "Do you know what happened to me today? The clerk at the gas station wouldn't take my credit card because I left my purse at work with my identification in it; and she knows me. Heck, she sees me nearly every day—but she's a real grouch anyway."
>
> *Second Person:* "That sucks, but do you know what my boss said to me today? He informed me that I was always late from lunch and told me in no uncertain terms that I would either be on time or lose my job. He knows that the traffic is horrible at lunch, and he's always gone more than an hour. I should just tell him to stuff it!"

Third Person: "Your day was nearly as bad as mine. I had a damn cop stop me for almost nothing. Everyone in traffic was changing lanes, and just because I cut in front of him, he gave me a ticket. That's my third one this year, and my insurance costs are going to go through the roof as a result. These damn cops should be out catching real criminals, not honest, tax-paying citizens."

First Person: "Life sucks. Is your husband still being a jerk? Oh, but you know, speaking of insurance rates, my insurance company canceled my insurance just because I was late with their payment. Then that *blankity blank* that ran into me led to a fine for my not having insurance. And on top of that, they blamed me for the accident, and it wasn't my fault!"

By now you get the idea. These people gather to share their cookie stories, and that is largely what their social life is all about. If you want to have some fun, step up to the cookie keepers and point out how wonderful life is. You might even explain the blame game and cookie-keeper philosophy, but make sure you have a plan for a quick retreat.

Cookie Keepers

Cookie keepers choose, whether or not they want to admit it, to hold tightly to the blame game. An otherwise productive and joyful life is thrown away in exchange for the "Don't you feel sorry for me?" interactions. That is another part of the cookie-keeper game. To belong to their group, you must be willing to be understanding and sympathetic. It's okay to top the cookie of another with a more unpleasant cookie of your own, but not if you fail to recognize the poor, picked-on nature of the other cookie keeper.

A dear friend of mine grew up in a codependent family relationship, one of those Melody Beattie so aptly defines in her books such as *Codependent No More*. It's the relationship most of us know something about, for we probably heard many of those conditional statements growing up. They are ones that go like this: "If you loved me, you would _____. If you had any respect for me, you would not _____. I did this for you; is it too much to expect _____ from you? I think if you cared about me, you would _____" And so forth. You fill in the blanks. Beattie sets out several criteria for recognizing codependence. "Codependents are the people who consistently, and with a great deal of effort and energy, try to force things to happen," she says. She continues:

> We control in the name of love. We do it because we're
> "only trying to help." We do it because we know best how
> things should go and how people should behave. We do it be-
> cause we're right and they're wrong. We control because we're
> afraid not to do it. We do it because we don't know what else
> to do. We do it to stop the pain. We control because we think
> we have to. We control because we don't think. We control
> because controlling is all we can think about. Ultimately we
> may control because that's the way we've always done things.
> Tyrannical and dominating, some rule with an iron hand. . . .
> Others do their dirty work undercover. They hide behind a
> costume of sweetness and niceties, secretly going about their
> business—OTHER PEOPLE'S BUSINESS.

Two of the keystone elements in all of this codependency are, according to Beattie, "Suffering people's consequences for them" and "Solving people's problems for them." In other words, there is a real quid pro quo in cookie sharing, and it too is at least somewhat based on codependent patterns.

My friend gave up her codependent behavior and threw all of her cookies away. She chose to become self-empowered and has made wonderful strides in the process. If you asked her, she would tell you that life is a miracle, and she is very happy today. Still, her sister, with whom she has always been very close, has not budged. Her sister carries all the cookies she can and spends nearly every moment sharing them. Despite soft approaches at trying to turn on a light in the sister's head, my friend now finds herself in that place where many who refuse to play these games eventually arrive. It is hard to change when those you love the most are fixed in ways that steal your power. My friend has decided that the next time her sister plays the blame game, she will say something to end this behavior. You see, when you stop saving your cookies and get on with taking responsibility for everything in your life, your life improves. When that happens, you lose any and all desire to be a cookie keeper.

*Self-responsibility means taking responsibility for everything
in your life, even those events or people that do not in
any way seem to be your problem or responsibility.*

Often the people who most antagonize us are the ones we need most to teach us what we want to learn. My mother used to say, "Birds of a feather flock together." Call it that, or call it simple attraction, anger attracts anger, hostility attracts hostility, love attracts love, and so forth. As I mentioned earlier, what we resist we tend to become. When we see something in someone we do not like, we need to be careful, for often they are mirrors of ourselves. What we dislike in them is likely to be a behavior of our own. When we are alert to this, it's quite easy to do something remarkable, something that truly changes our own reality. Let me digress a minute.

Self-Responsibility

When I lived in Las Vegas, Nevada, my local post office was always jammed with patrons. They all seemed in a hurry, and the clerks were absolutely rude. Many times heated arguments erupted between patrons and staff. I decided to try a little experiment. *What would happen if I just smiled and mentally beamed light to all of these people?* I wondered.

Every day for at least two weeks when I stopped to pick up my mail, I did my best to focus light on all. One day, the oldest and grouchiest of the postal clerks, whose line I was queued in, looked up and said, "Hello, Dr. Taylor." There was a smile on his face and cheer in his voice. From that day forward, every clerk in the office spoke and smiled, laughed and joked with me. Everything had changed. They were still snippy with other patrons for a while, but the smile and light had paid off. Somehow, unconsciously even, they identified me with warmth and love. Within a few months, this post office and its employees were as warm and friendly as any I have ever visited.

It is amazing what a little unconditional love can do. We are all capable of coaching or cheering on our friends and family, but when it comes to strangers, particularly those we think of as rude, it is often another matter. It doesn't have to be. This is just another way to do good deeds.

Again, self-responsible means taking responsibility for everything in your life. That does not mean you're in charge of your environment and in control of all the stimuli you encounter. It does mean that you're in charge of your own inner environment and you begin to make choices—true choices that are healthy and wise. The so-called bad luck is seen through a different lens. In fact, there's a story about luck that I like to tell, because it illustrates well just how limited our judgments can be. First, however, to frame the story, let me tell you about one of my favorite country songs. The song titled "Unanswered Prayers" tells of a young man who falls in love with a girl in high school. He prays nightly that she will see him and love him in return. She marries another man, and years pass. He eventually meets a woman who turns out to be the real woman of his dreams. A few more years pass, and he receives an invitation to a high school reunion. At the reunion he sees the sweetheart who married another. She has aged early, is nasty and bitter, and in other ways is totally unattractive. He looks at his wife and says, "Thank God for unanswered prayers!"

"Thank God for unanswered prayers!"

So here is the story.

Luck

An old rancher back in the Civil War days was just barely getting by. His wife had died giving birth to his only son, and he himself was somewhat crippled with arthritis. His son, therefore, did most of the work around the ranch. Now, this rancher was a really nice man, and everyone in town liked him.

One day, the boy was out tilling the ground when lightning struck near the mules. The mules bolted, and the old harness could not hold them. The harness broke, and the mules ran off.

Without the mules, the rancher and his son would not be able to get their crops in, and they were barely making ends meet as it is was. The whole town turned out to commiserate. "Such bad luck," they said.

But the old farmer said, "Good luck, bad luck; who knows?"

Good luck, bad luck; who knows?

The next day the mules came running home, and behind them came a whole herd of wild horses. The farmer and his son seized the opportunity because horses were worth a lot of money. Armies on both sides of the Civil War were paying a lot of money for horses. They ran outside and opened the corral gates. When the horses and mules were inside, they closed the gates.

This time the whole town came out to congratulate them. "Such good luck!" they said. But the farmer just said, "Good luck, bad luck; who knows?"

The next day the son went out to break the horses, as nobody would buy a horse he could not ride. However, the very first horse he mounted simply sunfished and switched over. (This means that he went up facing west and came down facing east and then reared completely over backward.) The boy was lucky he wasn't more seriously hurt, just a broken arm and collarbone. This time the whole town came out to say, "Such bad luck."

The old farmer simply said, "Good luck, bad luck; who knows?"

The very next day, the army marched through town and conscripted every able-bodied man. Of course they did not take the farmer's son, because his arm and collarbone were broken. The whole town turned out again: "Such good luck."

The old farmer simply said, "Good luck, bad luck; who knows?"

The army was heading to Shiloh. Not many lived through that battle. You just never know what is good luck and what is bad luck. But when your bones are broken, you tend to think only of the pain, the inconvenience, the discomfort, and so on.

I was first told this story many years ago. Recently I learned it was actually a Sufi story and that Jonathan Robinson wrote a poem based on it. That poem, titled "The Old Man," is a slightly different version of the story above. In honor of the true story, here is the poem:

Once long ago, there lived an old man.
He had no money. He had no plan.
All that he had was a horse oh so grand
and he and his horse lived off the land.

The King offered riches for this horse oh so fine,
"I'll give you money if you'll make your horse mine."
But the old man said, "My horse will not be sold.
He lives with me. He lives free and bold."

Then one day the horse was plain gone.
"The horse has been stolen," the townsfolk cried on.
The old man said, "Friends, don't look so sad,
Though the horse may be gone that may not be so bad."

"You foolish old man, look what you've done.
You had a fine horse and now you have none.
A curse it is and a curse it will be.
You shouldn't have let your horse wander free!"

The horse soon returned with others by its side.
There were 12 now of beauty and pride.
The townsfolk said, "Old man, you were right.
You are blessed to have horses of unearthly delight!"

"I have now 12 horses, yes, that is true,
But that does not mean I am blessed with them too.
It is too soon to judge; who knows what will be?
Try not to make stories from the little you see."

As it came to pass, the old man's only son
Tried riding a horse, just for fun.
Yet he broke both his legs while playing this game
And the townsfolk cried, "Oh, what a shame!"

The old man said, "Friends, don't speak so soon.
You hear just one note, yet you sing an entire tune.
Who's to say what the future may hold?
My son's legs are broken, but the future lies untold."

Soon there was a war, and the young men of town
Were all sent to fight and were shot down.
But the old man's son was saved from this plight.
He had broken his legs; he was forced not to fight.

And the townsfolk cried out, "Again you were right!"
But the old man replied, "Have you no sight?
Only God knows what is and will be.
To live and let live is to live and live free."

To live and let live is to live and live free.

Either way, poem or story, the moral is clear: What often appears to be bad luck simply is not. Most of us, if honest, have everything we need right now—and now is our only certainty. If we choose to live in "now" with a gratitude attitude, taking what comes to us as the old farmer might, we'd be happier and live longer, healthier lives. That is just a fact. Why would anyone choose otherwise?

Humankind is unique. We all have the ability to think about the future. What about tomorrow? What if _____? (You fill in the blank.) All of this is worry over possibilities that we might actually be creating because we worry over them. It is clear that there is no pragmatic value in keeping cookies, playing the blame game, or disenfranchising ourselves while poisoning our bodies with chemicals on account of so-called synthetic threats.

The Zen Master

Before we leave the subject of "now," allow me to share two more stories with you. This one I heard years ago from a friend who did not know where it came from. It is about a Zen master who made it a habit at noontime to meditate while he walked in the gardens. On this particular day, he became so engrossed in his meditation that he wandered far into the jungle, where he met a hungry tiger. Well, our Zen master did what any Zen master would do, which is to attend to the urgency of the moment. He fled as fast as he could with the hungry tiger in pursuit. Soon he came to the edge of a sheer cliff, but with a hungry tiger about to eat him, he jumped over the edge. On the way down he grabbed the only thing jutting out from the cliff, a small tree. There he hung on as he heard a roar from below. Now, there was a hungry tiger above and a hungry tiger below. Just then the small tree began to pull out of the ground. He looked to his right. Nothing. He looked below. Nothing. He looked to his left. A beautiful strawberry. He picked the strawberry, and it was the best fruit he'd eaten in his life.

I have told this story many times in seminars around the world. Sometimes I have added things that might go through the minds of many: "Oh, I love strawberries, but I'm allergic to them," or we might fret those last precious moments of "now" away in panic, fear, and blame: "Why me, God?"

There are as many divisible units in "now" as there are in infinity, mathematically speaking. Living fully in the moment allows us to enjoy life with awe. The moral of the story is, be mindful—you will find the strawberries.

Look for the strawberries!

After I told this story to an audience in Malaysia, a fellow approached me during a break and asked if I knew the entire story.

"I thought that was the entire story."

"No," he said. "Would you like to know it?"

We sat down and had coffee while he related the story that he said comes from Paramahansa Yogananda. It seems that the Zen master, when confronted with the tigers, was actually hanging from a small apple tree while mice were digging away the light soil that the tree was rooted in. The story cuts away to a picture of the event hanging in a gallery. There spectators are viewing the art, when one speaks up, "Look at that stupid fellow. He's selfishly indulging his senses while blind to his circumstances." The story then returns to the Zen master. Another tiger runs onto the scene, and now there are two tigers above. The Zen master enjoys his apple, and pretty soon he sees vultures circling overhead. The two tigers have fought and killed each other. The mice see the shadow of the birds and flee. Below a herd of deer comes down to drink from the brook, and the tiger below sets off in pursuit of them. In short, what seemed like dire circumstances fixed themselves or were fixed by some power above.

The Power of Good Deeds

Years ago a young woman came to me for help. To maintain confidentiality, I will invent a name for her. I'll call her Mary. This young woman in her late 30s had a history of self-mutilation and suicidal behavior. She came in for pastoral counseling, and I agreed to see her only if her psychiatrist agreed and was kept fully informed. That issue out of the way, her first appointment was made. My secretary brought me her file, including the pre-process forms I used. As I reviewed her information, I was taken by the fact that one of her prior therapists was a famous psychiatrist. I thought to myself, *And what on earth am I to do if this person couldn't help her?*

During her first session, the terms of our arrangement were agreed upon. I would see her for ten weeks, once a week, and my conditions and requirements had to be kept. She agreed, and the session began, or perhaps more appropriately, she began sobbing and wailing. An hour passed, with nothing but tears to show for it. Few words could I understand amidst the sobbing. "Until next week," I said, and we parted.

I thought about her for the entire week and decided to try something totally new, at least for me and for that time (circa 1990). I theorized that all the excessive crying was simply her attention-seeking mechanism combined with true feelings of despair, but to get past that, we had to dispense with the wailing. I took a mirror that had been given to me by a cosmetic-surgeon friend, and which I had used for years to show, as he did, just how uneven the halves of our faces are (left versus right). Brain hemisphere dominance theories suggest a correspondence, so this was in keeping with my research and work.

When Mary visited in week two, she again began crying. I placed the mirror in front of her, explained as nicely as I could that she had to maintain some composure for me to help, told her to look at herself while she cried, and then said to let me know when she stopped. I stepped out of the office. Soon she opened the door. As I began to sit down, she started weeping again, so once again I exited. After three or four repetitions that admittedly took more than half of our time together, she stopped the sobbing and began talking. Her story was a sad one, about a child who was neglected in favor of a younger sibling who was smarter and prettier. Her early relationships with men were equally sad, but not out of the realm of what happens to psychologically well-balanced people.

When we were finished speaking for the day, it was clear that Mary had dwelled on all the bad, shared her cookies all too willingly, each time probably exaggerating them, and otherwise remained almost fixated on the worst possible future—in her case, becoming a bag lady in Las Vegas.

I gave Mary her homework, as part of our agreed terms. She was to do one good turn for someone, anyone, every day. She was to record the good deed in her journal just before going to sleep, focus on how the deed made her feel, and imagine how it made the recipient feel. The deed could be anything, as simple as holding a door for someone or as emotionally demanding as helping a colleague she didn't like. She was to bring the journal with her each week when she visited me.

The following week we reviewed her journal entries and her thoughts and feelings regarding each. Admittedly, some of her first week's good deeds were pretty weak, but a couple of them provided an opportunity to draw out the difference in how it made Mary feel, as well as how she might have felt if she had been the recipient. Her homework for the remaining weeks was simple: two good deeds every day and recorded per the earlier instructions.

Mary's perspective changed. Her focus moved from bad things to good things. It was that simple. There is nothing more eloquent than just saying it how it is. Armed with a positive outlook and an eye for opportunities to do good deeds, and supported with what I call a warm, fuzzy feeling that comes from helping others, Mary began to reinforce her own worth and find joy in living. It wasn't long before her medication was cut back and then eliminated. Mary found meaning in life.

The Warm, Fuzzy Feeling

I suggest to you that the real meaning in life comes from what you give, not from what you take. As Wayne Dyer puts it in his book *The Power of Intention,* purpose is not about vocation—it's about service! I believe that the warm, fuzzy feeling we derive from a true service experience—going to the aid of another in need—is the best feeling we can have when we put our head on the pillow each night. Gerald Jampolsky, M.D., has observed in his attitudinal healing centers that when a person goes to the aid of another, even otherwise intractable pain disappears.[2]

I am very fortunate to have many faces in my memories that give to me regularly. There was a time, before the prison study, which we'll return to in a moment, that my life was a wreck. Oh, I was successful by most standards—fancy cars, large homes, rental and recreation property, but my personal life was a total wreck. I didn't know how to have a personal relationship unless there was something in it for me. Some of the people around me accused me of changing women as often as most men change shirts. My only life definitions were money and power. From the outside I might have looked like I had something going, but on the inside I was a barren wasteland. I became agnostic, to say the least, cynical and paranoid, and seldom enjoyed a good night's sleep. Fortunately for me, something inside combined with circumstances to show me another choice, an alternative that at the very least held within it a sense of peace, balance, and even purpose.

As another aside, before continuing our prison story, when the centenarian population was studied to determine the reason behind their long lives and health, everyone expected something like "clean living and self-denial." It turned out that that wasn't the case. Indeed, the comedian George Burns could characterize many of the centenarians. They lived life without fear, full of joy and humor. What they all shared was a sense of purpose or connectedness to a Higher Power. The value of this sense of connectedness and purpose cannot be overstated. For me the warm, fuzzy feeling keeps me connected and provides purpose. It doesn't really matter what we do for a living, provided that we do it with integrity and for the good of others. A piece of Chinese antiquity I cherish is a book written on jade. The author, Su Dongpo, a very famous Chinese writer, says it this way: "We do not work or search for food but for truth." As President Woodrow Wilson stated over 1,000 years later:

> You are not here merely to make a living. You are here in order to enable the world to live more amply, with greater vision, with a finer spirit of hope and achievement.
>
> You are here to enrich the world, and you impoverish yourself if you forget this errand.

Forgiveness Messages

But let us get back to the inmate population at the Utah State Prison. To undo the blame in order to produce self-responsible and, therefore, self-empowered persons, and to move away from the anger-fear loop, I decided on three messages that to this day we include on every InnerTalk program we publish. The three messages: *I forgive myself, I forgive all others,* and *I am forgiven.*

We also included statements in first person ("I," not "you," phrases), because subliminal information is processed from the inside out and becomes our words in our stream of consciousness, affirmations designed to build self-esteem and gratitude. At that time, the mid-1980s, the idea of forgiveness having a therapeutic value was new. Since then, many studies, journals, and books have been written about the power of forgiveness.

Okay, what happened with our inmate population? The program worked. The results impressed everyone. The magic bullet, forgiving, together with general affirmations of well-being, worked. The post-test indicated a meaningful result. (If you are interested in more detail, see Appendix B.) The Utah State Prison officials were as pleased as I, and they followed up by installing libraries of our InnerTalk programs in all of their facilities. When they wanted a program for, say, weight lifting, we did it. Not so the inmate would become stronger per se, but because every single program included the forgiveness messages together with self-esteem units. Other prisons copied the system, and to this day many inmates work with the technology. And me? I went on to a new career.

◦◉◦

In conclusion, when you forgive, you essentially undo the ability to blame. If there is nothing to blame, then you are in charge of your response to outside stimuli. There is less room for anger without blame. There is less to fear when you're empowered. The purely pragmatic point is that it works!

In the next chapter, we will take a more thorough look at subliminal information processing and some of the disinformation out there regarding it. Still, if you never use anything else from this book other than the forgiveness lesson, your life will change for the better—and that's a promise! For what it is worth, I want you to know that I had my own epiphanies along the way. I started out trying to fix people, such as the inmates. I soon learned something that Gerald Jampolsky says in his wonderful book *Teach Only Love.* That is this: we teach what we want to learn. I learned the value of life over time, not all at once; the purpose called service; and how to fix myself, not that there still isn't room for improvment. In fact, one day I decided that if forgiveness was so important, then my company's top-selling title at the time (some 20 years ago), *Forgiving and Letting Go,* should be free. It is free to this day, and you can go to **www.eldontaylor.com** and get your copy right now.

CHAPTER 10

◦◉◦◉◦◉◦

THE NATURE OF A CONTROVERSY

*"A 'no' uttered from deepest conviction is better
and greater than a 'yes' merely uttered to please,
or what is worse, to avoid trouble."*

— MAHATMA GANDHI

When I began my research at The University of Utah library, there was little controversy surrounding the idea of subliminal communication. Early research suggested that this information might even be prioritized by the mind above normally processed verbal information. Since then, this idea has been repeatedly demonstrated, particularly by cognitive psychologists using implicit/ explicit memory studies. In this research words are paired, and subjects study the pairing. For example, the word *house* is paired with *chair, green* with *tree,* and so forth. One set of subjects reviews the words with full conscious awareness and attention, seeing the word *chair* followed by the word *house,* while another group receives the word match subliminally, so the word *chair* is seen but the word *house* is presented subliminally. These studies repeatedly demonstrate higher matches for the group that receives the subliminal match word. Current research, however, shows that some attention is required for these effects to be seen.[1]

The advantage to subliminal affirmations is obvious. I often demonstrate this in seminars, as I pointed out earlier, by asking the participants, "Who would like to make a million dollars this year?"

All hands go up. Then I instruct the audience to say to themselves with meaning, "I'm going to make a million dollars this year!" Within just a few seconds, smiles begin to shine from faces in the audience as they get back their true inner belief: "Sure, what are you going to do, rob a bank?" The fact is that to make a million dollars, we must believe we can. If Bill Gates were in the audience, his goal would not be a million dollars, because that is far too little for him. No, his expectation and true inner belief would put a much higher number in place.

I am going to make a million dollars this year.

Telling ourselves we can or will do something, such as losing weight, has value, but that value is mitigated by our own true inner belief. Our inner belief must change for change to occur. When subliminal information is processed, it enters our stream of consciousness. It literally becomes our own self-talk. In time it simply overwhelms a lot of the no/don't, I can't, and other information that is our chicken-yard learning. Soon we believe the message "I am good" instead of challenging it with such statements as "Good at what? Do you remember when?"

Truth Has No Percentages

However, the field of subliminal information processing was becoming controversial. At the height of the controversy, the famous civil lawsuit involving Judas Priest was tried. I was asked to look at the information by the plaintiff's attorneys, who had brought a wrongful death action against CBS (the publisher) and Judas Priest. I had testified as an expert witness before, but that did not prepare me for some of what followed my deposition and testimony in this case. There was definitely an orchestrated campaign to discredit witnesses and testimony that might argue subliminal information is not only perceived but also acted upon. In my instance, the press had some real fun. For example, I had friends phone and ask if I had seen the Joan Rivers show on CBS. I had not seen the show, so they informed me that I had been portrayed as a mail-order minister who was a high-school dropout. "Truth," I used to say when conducting lie-detection interviews, "knows no percentages. It is either complete or omitting. A substantial relevant omission is deception. No one wants their significant other to be 99 percent faithful. Truth is either 100 percent or it's not the truth."

The truth to the Joan River's statements may be literally correct, I still have not seen the show, but they are out of context and substantially omitting relevant information. As a senior in high school in my last semester and holding a perfect 4.0 (A) GPA, I was called into Reed Call's office, the principal of Granger High School. He informed me that since I had missed several days of school (I lived on my own and held at least one job while attending school to pay for board, room, clothing, and so forth) and the school was reimbursed one dollar a day for attendance, they could not graduate me. I would have to make up the lost dollars to the school by attending summer school. There was a month or so of high school left, and I had been offered a postgraduate scholarship if I graduated on schedule. As a hot-headed young 18-year-old, I basically told Mr. Call, whom I must admit I had no respect for based on other incidents, to put his diploma where the proverbial sun doesn't shine. I left the high school and never went back.

At the age of 25, I decided to return to school. I matriculated at Weber State University in Ogden, Utah. No high school equivalency such as the GED was required based on my admission test scores. Indeed, my scores on the College-Level Examination Program (CLEP) provided a year's worth of college credit. At the time, I thought I wanted to go to law school, so after three years at Weber, I applied to the University of the Pacific's McGeorge School of Law, and they had me take a college-equivalency examination at the university that again I passed. Things in my life changed about then, so I did not go to law school. The long and the short of it comes down to this. I invested thousands of dollars and hours in alternative-distance education, as well as weeklong intensives. Along the way, I earned a doctorate in psychology, became a Fellow in the American Psychotherapy Association, and became an ordained minister. My ministerial schooling at the University of Metaphysics (**www.metaphysics.com**) was among the best time and money I invested. It was a correspondence program conducted in a distance-learning format, so I suppose it is somewhat true: I am a mail-order minister who dropped out of high school.

Subliminal Influence

However, back to the Judas Priest trial. The case involved two young men who, after drinking a few beers while repeatedly playing the song "Better by You, Better Than Me" from the *Stained Class* album by Judas Priest, took a shotgun to the playground and shot themselves. (The full account is also provided in my book *Thinking Without Thinking*):

> Two teenage boys had difficulty adjusting to life. Ray had just split up with his girlfriend. James had just lost his job. Neither of them was blameless. Both of them were confused. For most young people, the approach to adulthood provides struggles. It should.
>
> Two days before Christmas, Ray gave James a gift of music. The music had particular significance. James had once collected the music of this particular artist, but when he found the music violated his Christian beliefs, he threw it all away.
>
> That was a few years before. James no longer pursued any religious affiliation. He had turned away from religion. Many people do at some point in their lives.
>
> On December 23rd, James received the album. The boys decided to play the album while they drank beer. The words and music of one song held their interest. They played it repeatedly. The lyrics in several songs encouraged suicide with such rhymes as "Leave this life with all its sin / It's not fit for living in."
>
> Picture these two young men, attractive, on the slight side—skinny, according to more than one description—unskilled, not doing well in school, anticipating a life of difficulty and with delusions of grandeur driven by frustration,

pretending to be mercenaries, or imagining themselves as heroes.

By mid-afternoon, the lyrics going around in their heads included, "Why do you have to die to be a hero?" The two looked at each other as though acting in some movie. The hero says, "Let's do it!" just before mayhem begins. One of the boys said, "Do it!" The two began chanting, "Do it." One of them grabbed a shotgun. They went out the bedroom window to the church playground. Ray placed a shotgun under his jaw. James chanted, "Do it!" Ray fired the gun. The blast stunned James. Ray was dead.

James lifted the gun, wet with blood. He said later that he trembled. He felt afraid. He could be blamed for Ray's death. He wondered why they had chanted, "Do it." He placed the gun under his own jaw. He pulled the trigger.

But James had failed to brace the shotgun. As he pulled the trigger, the gun lurched forward. The blast shot off the front of his face. It did not kill him. It left him severely wounded and disfigured. He lived for nearly three years.

After reviewing the case, I took the position, unpopular as it turned out to be, that the subliminal command "Do it!" was a causal factor in the double shooting. However, the point we are interested in here is not the details of the case. Rather, it is the birth of a scientific controversy. Prior to this case, Congressional hearings in 1984 had led to the most significant source of scientific controversy, which was simply whether or not a subliminal message could affect behavior. Lloyd Silverman said yes, and Howard Shevrin was doubtful.[2] In the Judas Priest case, Shevrin switched positions based on newer research and agreed with me: The subliminal "Do it" command was a causal factor.[3]

Questionable Science

You might wonder, *So what was the controversy?* A new study conducted by a marketing student on the influence of labels was being announced everywhere—and I do mean everywhere, from *Seventeen* magazine to prime-time news. This study purportedly proved that subliminal messages did not work to influence behavior. (Again, you can read all the details of this study and the Congressional hearings in my book *Thinking Without Thinking.*)

A psychologist I have great respect for supervised the study. Unfortunately, the study itself did not achieve what the media or the pundits who sided with CBS claimed it did. So you understand why it's necessary for me to go through the study in some detail.

By design, the study evaluated the influence of labels on the consumer. To do this, the doctoral student who set up the research project sought and obtained subliminal audiotapes from five different companies. The tapes were of two kinds, one to improve memory and one to build esteem. The labels on the tapes were then changed so that the esteem tapes were labeled memory and vice versa. The pretest instruments measured memory and esteem. After the test period, subjects were brought back and tested for actual improvement. Subjects who thought they were playing memory subliminal messages reported an improvement in memory, and subjects who believed they were listening to esteem messages reported an increase in their esteem. The instruments failed to identify a statistically meaningful change in either. Fair enough, at this point, to state a definite label influence, but how about a real effect regarding subliminal communication?

The five tape companies all claimed different methods and messages for their programs, including messages in the second person and messages in the first person. Audio analysis failed to recover messages on any of the programs. (Remember my Audio Forensic Labs test?)

The fact that audio messages were not recorded does not surprise me. According to an affidavit from the sound engineer of one major manufacturer of audio subliminal programs, messages were mixed 40 decibels (db) beneath the carrier (music or ocean sounds). This 40 db is beneath the theoretical limit of most players. In other words, the signal strength might be compared to the influence of a whisper two blocks away. It might be that the messages were not recoverable because the *secret* method used included such a mixing procedure. Other companies used questionable affirmations and in other ways produced material that differentiated one company from another. All shared the label "subliminal," but that certainly did not mean they were the "same."

Let me give you an example to clarify the importance of this difference. Assume a scientist pressurizes a trapped atmosphere to, say, ten atmospheric pressures, applies an exact electric charge, and then heats the result. To replicate this study, a researcher would determine the nature of the atmosphere that was trapped and replicate the process, including the exact degree of heat and electric current applied. Now assume that someone attempts to replicate the study by catching room atmosphere in a fishbowl and covering it with plastic wrap so it is trapped. He places a nine-volt battery inside the fishbowl and then heats it with a cigarette lighter. Hardly the same experiment. Let's now take it a step farther. Imagine that five fishbowl makers all use different elements but claim the same outcome. Is testing all five bowl makers the same as replicating the original study? The answer is clear: *No!* Even if one of the bowl makers has it right, the other four would contaminate the outcome.

So, we are not looking at a scientific study with a single variable. We are mixing multiple variables and coming up with a single conclusion—and that simply is not good science! Nevertheless, this study was in the media everywhere, and those testifying for CBS and Judas Priest were touting it almost as if it were the Holy Grail.

The long and the short of this case comes down to a few facts. Judas Priest admitted to putting subliminal content on some recordings but not this one. When the messages were demonstrated to be present, the counter argument was that it occurred only as a "coincidence of sound." CBS was fined more than once by the judge for impeding the discovery process and manipulating the press. It was CBS Records' own disclosure of the boys chanting, "Do it." CBS's own investigator, a former Scotland Yard detective, stated that he was unable to locate the original 24-track master and that he was never allowed to look in the CBS vault. (The original master was needed in order to prove the message was not a coincidence of sound). In a wrongful death action, intent must be demonstrated.

This was not a product liability suit, as would be the case with defective brakes on an automobile.

Subliminal Messages Do Influence Behavior

The result of the press attention and managed or manipulated media gave rise to the real scientific controversy. Since then, the power of subliminal messages to influence behavior has been admitted by some of the most outspoken persons defending the position of CBS. Even the *Skeptical Enquirer,* a science journal that has a history of debunking many things later proven to be true, admits evidence for behavior changes due to subliminal stimuli,[4] and they published a number of scientific articles supposedly debunking the subliminal influence during and following the Judas Priest trial. The definitive work of Robert Bornstein and his meta-analysis approach show clearly that a properly delivered (signal strength) psychoactive message (affirmation) can and does influence behavior.[5] The fact of the matter is, as Bornstein put it to me in a telephone conversation following a television filming for the Discovery Channel, the effects of subliminal stimuli on humans, including behavior, is so robust in the literature that you have got to wonder where individuals who deny it have been in the last ten years.

The research on InnerTalk includes over a dozen double-blind studies conducted by independent researchers at leading institutions throughout the world and on a number of domains ranging from attention deficit hyperactive disorder (ADHD) to depression (see Appendix A for more information). The model is simple and was first put forward by Albert Ellis.[6]

The A-B-C model, as it is called, is graphically depicted as follows:

$$A \longrightarrow B \longrightarrow C$$

(activating event)   (belief)   (consequence: emotional and behavioral)

An activating event, stimulus, or verbal affirmation affects belief, which equals emotional and behavioral consequences. It is easy to see this rather linear in and out when looking at the negative input in our lives, and it works more or less in the same way with respect to the positive. Ellis coined a term for negative self-talk that is best known as ANTS: automatic negative thoughts. I like this term because it is easy to imagine ants tearing down your positive thoughts and carrying in the negative. Perhaps the next time the ants are bugging you, you can do what I do. Just imagine a little ant bait and let them feed. You can simply follow a negative thought with something like "And then what?" Eventually, the "then whats" lose their power. Even a "then you die" is not threatening when you remember that you are a creation of the Divine—but back to our story.

The Danger Message

During the Judas Priest trial, I was asked if I had ever conducted a research design that indicated a person would kill himself as a result of a subliminal message. "Of course not" had to be my answer. No scientist I know of would even consider doing such a thing, at least I hope not. Then an idea came to me. What if a person received a subliminal message of danger?

A pilot study was arranged. My daughter, Hillarie, who was working on a science project for high school, accepted my suggestion and obtained the appropriate guidance and permissions from all involved.

Group A listened to the sounds of the ocean with three subliminal information deliveries, approximately one minute apart. The messages were "DANGER, DANGER, WATCH OUT!—AH-H-H-G-H! DANGER!" The messages were recorded and delivered simultaneously in both forward and reversed speech. Group B listened to the same ocean track with the message "People are walking."

Both groups listened to the audio programs for four minutes, with earphones, while their body responses were monitored for changes in breathing, blood pressure, the electrical resistance of their skin, and the moisture at the ends of their fingers. A four-needle polygraph, the same instrument used as a "lie detector," recorded these responses.

After the four-minute trial, each subject responded to a questionnaire that included a request to report any particular reveries, feelings, or thoughts that occurred during the trials. Only then did an assistant discover and reveal to the subject which group he or she was in.

All five of those in group A responded with gross reactions or changes in the measurements of body function coinciding with the delivery of the subliminal "danger" message. Those in the B group had no such response. This suggests a danger-stimulus recognition. The bodies of the subjects in group A responded as though an actual danger existed. So did their minds. Three of the five individuals in group A reported reveries of killing or being killed. A fourth person reported feeling extremely upset. The fifth said she was too occupied by what the experimenters were doing to notice her thoughts. (The experimenters were doing very little.) Psychological theory has categories of fantasy formation. Our response to danger, the fight/flight response, can generate compelling fantasies.

When a person feels threatened, fight/flight gives rise to thoughts of this nature. Killing is fight oriented, and death may be flight oriented. Many deal with fear, in fantasy, by neutralizing the source of the fear—even if it means killing. Dying, on the other hand, means escape to many. Of five normal, healthy teenagers, four had thoughts of killing or dying. The fifth apparently "blanked out." This came from one listening, in a pleasant and sober state, to a few repetitions of a single, simple, subliminal message for a few minutes.

Those who heard the message "People are walking" had reveries that went like this: "I was at a sunny beach, and there were a lot of people."

I have since posted this study together with all needed materials, including downloadable sound files, as an academic challenge at **www.progressiveawareness.org**. No one has run the study with a different outcome.

Today, the science of subliminals is still hyped and poorly understood by many, but it is a true science with valid merits. It truly can assist in enabling individuals to overcome their doubts and fears and negative input that all too often create self-imposed limitations.

Madonna

It is not uncommon for musical groups to use subliminal information, as I suggested earlier. In 1991, I was contacted by WNCI radio regarding satanic messages in a Madonna recording. Not only were the messages there, but also her people later admitted to putting them there for publicity purposes. Here are some of those messages delivered in poetic format:

> In the midnight smoke of yellow
> Hear my melodies
> Hail to the family
> It must be unknown
> Hail hallelujah my position . . .

The influence media has over our thoughts and actions is worth spending just another moment on. For years I have had a proverbial pet peeve against the selling of illness. For example, every year we are told through the media, chiefly television, that the dreaded "gomboo" is coming to town. We are also told that we'll probably catch it, as if we were going to run down the street and catch a cold (notice those words, please). But that's okay, because there is a remedy, and when we take it we will be pampered in bed like the characters acting out the TV commercial.

We are all exposed to fancy cars with beautiful people paired with them, as if when we want something beautiful in our lives, or to be sexy and so forth, we need this product to obtain it. Most of us are aware of this kind of advertising, and still it can influence us.

There are general categories applied to the definition of subliminal communication through any media. Wolman sets out the categories this way:

Wolman's Categories

Professor Benjamin B. Wolman's modified categorization of subliminal stimuli divides descriptive values into four criteria of awareness and unawareness. The stimuli are as follows:

- Below the level of registration

- Above the level of registration but below the level of detection

- Above the level of detection and discrimination but below the level of identification*

- Below the level of identification only because of a defensive action[7]

*Using Wolman's categories,
our patented InnerTalk technology falls into category three.

Wolman, B.B. (1973)

Embeds such as those in the liquor advertisement illustrated and discussed in Chapter 6 may well fit into category 4. Messages such as those in Madonna and Judas Priest generally fit into category 3. A category 2 subliminal message may well be the type flashed on a screen, such as the reported popcorn and cola flashes in the infamous New Jersey theater instance. A category 1 is the message mixed at 40 db beneath the music when played on a stereo with a db limitation of 30.

In coming chapters, we will look at the nature of the mind and other influences that contribute to the makeup of the total human condition, including the so-called paranormal, but first let's take a look at another tool you can use to counteract mind programming—hypnosis.

CHAPTER 11

⊙◉⊙◈⊙◉⊙

PRACTICAL HYPNOSIS

"The empires of the future will be the empires of the mind."

— WINSTON CHURCHILL

As mentioned earlier, for years I practiced forensic hypnosis. I have used it with victims and with alleged perpetrators. I have seen the mind bring back incredible detail while a subject experienced hypnosis. In the homicide case that I spoke of earlier, for example, a man charged and convicted of the murder of his mother was able to detail precisely the events of the evening in question, despite his otherwise drugged stupor. We were able to verify his information, which provided an iron-tight alibi, and he was subsequently released from prison.

I have also used hypnosis for assisting others in improving their lives—from childbirth to weight loss, from priming behaviors to uncovering buried memories. I believe hypnosis to be an invaluable tool in anyone's self-improvement armamentarium, especially as this is something you can carry out on yourself—you can employ self-hypnosis to achieve your goals as opposed to having someone else hypnotize you.

Demystifying Hypnosis

First, let's demystify hypnosis. When called to testify in a court of law, hypnosis is defined according to two standards: objective and subjective states. The objective state is simply a slowed brain-wave activity. Instead of operating at our normal beta consciousness, we slip into alpha or even theta. Let me unpack that a bit and put some direct relevance on what it means:

- Normal consciousness is referred to in terms of brain-wave cycles as beta. This is a state equal to 15 cycles per second and up, typically 15 to 30 cycles per second.

- Below beta is alpha, a state typically thought of as represented by 8 to 14 cycles per second of brain-wave activity when measured by an electroencephalograph (EEG).

- Below alpha is theta, which is 4 to 7 cycles.

- Below that is delta.

Alpha and theta brain-wave patterns are those manifest when the subject is in hypnosis. These brain-wave cycles are also those present when sleeping, and perhaps this partially explains why so many hypnotists use the word *sleep*. Entering hypnosis is indeed similar in the sense that brain-wave activity follows the same pattern, and visualization while in hypnosis can be very much like the rapid eye movement (REM) experienced during sleep.

Now for the second measure, that of the subjective state—when in alpha, as stated earlier, you are hypersuggestible.

A number of studies have demonstrated the power of sleep learning. They show us that it is during those states we call REM, or the thresholds of falling asleep and waking up—all of which are also what we know as alpha-dominant brain-wave patterns—when we are particularly responsive to learning stimuli. I think of this state of activity and its accompanying association with accelerated learning and suggestibility, or hypnotic effects, as analogous to fencing material. When the brain is functioning in beta, perhaps under some stress at 30 cycles per second, the fencing material is very tightly woven (many lines per inch). When slowed down to 8 cycles per second, the fencing material is much more loosely woven (fewer lines per inch), and the result is simply a matter that more information can pass between the lines or gain entry to the other side of the fence. (See Figure 25).

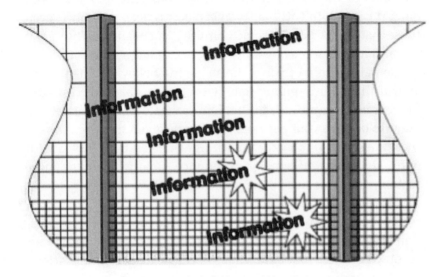

Figure 25

From the drawing, it should also be easy to see why so many meditators have used self-hypnosis to learn to quiet the mind, to open those supposed fence grids in an endeavor to "be still and know." Indeed, this altered state, whether called meditation or self-hypnosis, has been shown to positively affect the brain when done regularly for as little as 30 days. In one study, reported in November of 2012, meditation was shown to produce enduring changes in emotional processing.[1]

Other research has shown that meditation can cause fundamental changes in the brain, including new brain cells, axons, dendrites, and synapses. These studies showed dramatic brain alterations that are brought about due to quieting the mind. In fact, simply daydreaming, again an alpha-dominant state, increases creativity and probably brings about the same sort of brain changes.

Practical Uses of Hypnosis . . . and More!

Some of the most amazing things come through when you quiet the mind. In this state, you can access deep memories, even those that you decided at some point that you wanted to hide. You can also rewrite some of your own personal script—the script that is often at the root of your self-sabotaging behaviors. Many have argued that in a hypnotic state it is also possible to access your higher self, that part of you that knows whatever it is you need to know to become your personal best in any given situation. In fact, there are some simply amazing things that can be achieved with hypnosis. I have personally experienced many, but none more striking than this story that I will share with you.

The abbreviated version goes this way:

I once had a young woman come to me on the recommendation of her surgeon for pain management. She was in continuous chronic pain due to a back injury and repeated surgeries. After a couple of sessions, when it was time to return to normal consciousness, I suggested that I would count her up. However, she interrupted and informed me that there was a man who wished to speak with me. This man began speaking in a tongue I did not know. I recorded her speaking and later had the language department at The University of Utah inform me that it was an ancient Chinese dialect. The man speaking through my patient was informing me of a great battle that took place and some hidden scrolls that were tucked away in the Great Wall of China. The woman knew no Chinese, had never been around the language, and, for that matter, this ancient dialect was not generally spoken any longer even in China. (For the full story and many more like this that simply challenge our conventional view of the world, see my book *What Does That Mean?*)

Bottom line, I have often been asked for tools of change, and the two most powerful technologies that I know of are self-hypnosis and subliminal technology. Your mind dictates your life, at least from the perspective of your choices when dealing with all that life brings you. Your thoughts may actually belong to someone other than you. Perhaps you are only storing them so as to be prepared to act on them and buy, vote, feel, or emote on cue. Think of it this way—only someone concerned about the possibility of drowning buys a life preserver. Given that simple understanding, it's easy to see that most ads are based on informing you of your inadequacies or heightening your fears.

Hypnosis can be a powerful tool for uncovering all of the information stored in your mind, selectively choosing that which you no longer wish to store, and assisting in discarding it.

It is your mind, but odds are that not everything in there is of your choosing. But then, what exactly is this stuff we call *mind?*

CHAPTER 12

◈◉◈◉◈◉◈

MIND IS NOT
A LOCAL EVENT

*"All I have seen teaches me to trust the
Creator for all I have not seen."*

— RALPH WALDO EMERSON

Mind. Consciousness. What is it we mean when we use these words? Bruce Lipton once told me of an experiment where dividing cells were scraped with a tongue depressor; half remained in a petri dish in the laboratory, and the other half were taken five miles away. On cue, the cells in the lab were shocked with low-voltage current. The cells five miles away immediately responded as if they were in the dish back in the lab. Cell consciousness? Indeed, according to Lipton's book *The Biology of Belief,* not only are the cells conscious, but they also respond to thoughts and beliefs—and the "they" in cells includes the DNA. The DNA can be "turned on" by belief, or, in the words of Dr. Ernest Lawrence Rossi, "The mind drives the body, which drives the genetic code." The implications lead Rossi to this conclusion: "The dynamics of gene expression and brain plasticity can be initiated within the time frame of a typical psychotherapy session."

"The mind drives the body, which drives the genetic code."

Cleve Backster became famous overnight, not for his lie-detection school or his special version of the polygraph, but for his plants. Headlines ran: "Your Plants May Tell on You." Cleve wired a philodendron to the galvanic skin response (GSR) readings of a polygraph. Three subjects passed through the room, looking first at the goldfish in the bowl next to the plant, then at a Bunsen burner heating water, and then at the plant. The same three passed through a second time, but this time the last one took a goldfish and dropped it in boiling water. The plant responded as though it were conscious, aware and even shocked at what happened. Then, in a stroke of genius, Cleve mixed up the order in which the subjects entered the room. Every time the fish killer entered the room, the plant responded. The plant was apparently identifying the perpetrator, perhaps in fear. What do you think?

There is a tremendous new interest in the study of consciousness. For years the subject was taboo in science, simply because it was seen as inherently unverifiable. That is, your consciousness and my consciousness are uniquely subjective. Science is all about objective and verifiable inquiry. Indeed, the scientific method requires that. Today, in part due to investigations directed at artificial intelligence and new experimental designs, consciousness is again being examined.

What is consciousness? Language is often thought to be the tool of consciousness and evidence for the kind of consciousness that makes humans different from monkeys. Indeed, language has often been referred to as the "jewel of cognition." Some scientists have argued that Neanderthal man possessed advanced talking ability. This assertion is largely based upon a neck bone found in 1988, which allegedly (due to its shape alone) allowed for vocal articulation.[1] Other scientists argue for a more recent origin to speech—recent, in this sense, being between 50 and 100 thousand years ago. By contrast, early origin theorists date the beginning of language at more than 2 million years ago.

What Is Consciousness?

The evolution and history of language have a bearing on certain philosophical issues where consciousness is concerned. For example, take any date for the first appearance of language. For fun, let's just assume some hairy bipedal creature that has never spoken. Is this creature conscious? Conscious in the sense that humans are conscious? Now one day the creature utters some meaningful form of speech. Not a grunt or guttural sound, as all animals do, but some form—beginning—of speech. Is the creature now conscious?

What is the difference between the consciousness of animals and the consciousness of humans? What is intended by distinguishing between the two conscious forms as different, and why? If a primate species shows the ability to learn, remember, and associate learnings, some insist this is evidence for reason. Most flatly refuse to recognize it as such. Is it possible that by recognizing consciousness as worthy and ripe for study that man's consciousness will lose its unique, elevated status? What precisely is it that one means by consciousness, anyway?

Certainly reason preceded language. It would be rather odd if it were the other way around. Still, that's an interesting thought.

Some people seem to reason only with the tools of their language. In other words, their reason is limited by the rules and definitions of their language. Plus, there is some argument in favor of certain language structure as having greater or lesser faculties for developing logical thinking. Literal languages such as German, for example, tend to encourage the development of logical thinkers. However intriguing this may be, it still seems reasonable that reason preceded the conceptualization and development of speech. As such, one is hard-pressed to limit the consciousness of a species on the basis of sound patterns called speech.

It gets still tougher. Sound patterns that resemble speech are uttered by so-called nonconscious animals, such as whales and dolphins. So, what is consciousness?

Is it a matter of wakefulness? No, it can't be just that, for one can be a conscious being and still be asleep. Is consciousness memory? According to the experiments of Cleve Baxter, plants exhibit memory. Since science abandoned the study of consciousness years ago, the problems inherent in describing consciousness have proliferated during the interim. The advent of animal studies, plant studies, and synthetic or artificial intelligence has greatly complicated the matters of consciousness . . . or perhaps simplified them.

For most people, parts of the left brain handle language. Brain hemispheric studies, including the now popular positron-emission tomography (PET) scans show that the right ear sends acoustic information to the left hemisphere. According to Marc Hauser (formerly of Harvard University) and Karin Andersson of Radcliff College in Cambridge, rhesus monkeys "display a similar cerebral setup, with the left half of the brain often taking responsibility for vocalizations intended to signal aggression."[2] If that is true, does it mean that the anatomical evidence for language processing is evidence for consciousness in the sense that we normally think of humankind's consciousness. If not, what are the differences?

For some, *mind* equals *brain*. But for many, *mind* is a more general term that refers to the processes handled by the brain. Therefore, mind is often used interchangeably with *consciousness*. Is *mind* equal to *brain?* The chief area of inquiry offering evidence one way or another to answer this question is a discipline often held in low regard. Still, literally thousands of laboratory experiments in scientific parapsychology demonstrate that many aspects of mind cannot be reduced to anatomical or material brain. For example, data clearly supports the "reality" of telepathy, clairvoyance, and psychokinesis. Indeed, although controversial, recent Russian DNA research explains much of this phenomena (clairvoyance, intuition, spontaneous healing, and so on) and proposes that DNA can be influenced by words and frequencies, not unlike the claim of Rossi.[3]

The biographies of some of the world's most respected people also provide a richer picture than can be found even in science. Famous individuals throughout history have provided numerous reports of their experiences with the so-called paranormal. Throughout the world and even in America's capital, Washington, D.C., there exist numerous reports, ranging from Abraham Lincoln's ghost wandering the White House to the Reagan administration's use of psychics. The point is simple. Whether it is from the genius of Einstein or the laboratory of a modern parapsychologist, mind is not equal to brain! What does that mean with respect to consciousness?

Consciousness Evolving

A wonderful *Star Trek* adventure I can remember had the *Enterprise* actually forming its own consciousness and then creating a new life-form. Somehow, as Mr. Data explained, the activity of the starship's computers and records began to take on a "more than the sum of the parts" activity, form its own neural network and so forth. Will machines ever become conscious?

This was the headline in a *Science News* publication: "Simulated Creatures Evolve and Learn." The article, by Richard Lipkin, cited the work of Karl Sims, who "devised a simulated evolutionary system in which virtual creatures compete for resources in a three-dimensional arena. . . . The creatures, resembling toy-block robots, enter one-on-one contests in which they vie for control of a desired object—an extra cube. Winners—deemed more fit—reproduce, while losers bear no offspring. Sims endows the virtual environment with physical parameters, such as gravity and friction, and restricts behaviors to plausible physical actions."[4] Sims believes that it may be easier to evolve virtual entities with intelligent behavior than to create them from scratch. Artificial-intelligence researchers have long sought to develop the so-called thinking machine. Unlike Sims, most begin by attempting to model the computer after the patterns of man. For some, this is the neural model of the brain, while for others it is the deductive/inductive model of reason. Perhaps Sims's method is more humanlike than the other two. Humankind is thought to have evolved. Does this help us understand consciousness? What about the collective consciousness? Will machines soon be contributing to this field of consciousness? Will a machine ever dream?

The "Genius Hypothesis," advanced by Ervin Laszlo,[5] asserts that the minds "of unusually creative people are in spontaneous, direct, though usually not conscious, interaction with other minds *in the creative process itself.*" Laszlo's paper sheds light on the "archetypal experience" described by Carl Jung while using history, physics, psychology, artistic production, and cultural development to clearly suggest the strong possibility (in my opinion, the only real possibility) that not only do minds communicate, but they do so at a distance as well!

Not only do minds communicate,
but they do so at a distance as well!

Is the collective, or the shared, consciousness experience an independent consciousness? Is it possible that unique (individual) conscious entities participate as transceivers, sending and receiving, and that the total of consciousness is this collective? Does the collective have a plan, a will? Does it dream? Or is it just a repository? Does it have a neural network or some analogous something that we might refer to as a nonspatial field? It's not organic or silicone, is it?

Conscious of Consciousness?

Perhaps consciousness is something that has to do with being conscious of consciousness. Are monkeys truly conscious of being conscious? Could they even entertain the idea of consciousness without an object? Or consciousness as a character in someone else's dream? Does a monkey ask itself if it really exists?

Is that a fair direction to take our questions regarding consciousness? After all, are we not likely to be forced to admit the notion of "devolution" if we do? Are there not altogether too many homo sapien sapiens on the planet who don't give the proverbial "hoot" about who they are or where they came from? How many of these people ask the question, "Do I really exist?" Will silicone ask the question, "Who am I?" The Japanese have already built a "Darwin machine." The artificial brain uses an evolving neural network. Hugo de Garis, a researcher in the field of artificial intelligence, says the purpose is to produce a silicone brain with more than one billion artificial neurons.

Science News says this machine "will come in the form of a neural network and will exist within a massively parallel computer. To create such a complex system, the researchers will have the network build itself. 'Cellular automata,' each one a distinct computer program, will actually forge their own linkages."

This approach, called "evolutionary engineering," provides for the growth of the silicone brain via connections. "The neural net grows when cellular automata send 'growth signals' to each other, then connect via synapses."[6] (And you thought genetic engineering was something to wonder about.)

Defining consciousness turns out to be a process somewhat akin to searching for the core of an onion. Revisiting consciousness is more than a philosophical exercise or a scientific inquiry. It is a duty, even a moral imperative, to reevaluate the nature of consciousness, for this inherently devises the strategy by which humankind treats itself and all life. For me, and I suspect for countless others, many changes are necessary for the human race to actualize the highest of its potentials. As in history, most certainly some of these changes will be brought about by difficult times. I am reminded of something Martin Luther King, Jr., said: "I can never be what I ought to be until you are what you ought to be . . ." King pointed out that it is precisely the interrelated fabric of life that each of us is interdependent upon.

*"I can never be what I ought to be
until you are what you ought to be . . ."*

— MARTIN LUTHER KING, JR.

Perhaps it is the interrelated nature of all life, consciousness itself, upon which we are interdependent. Perhaps, just perhaps, humankind will only know its highest, most noble self when it offers the deepest respect for all life. Perhaps the invigorated enthusiasm searching for a firm hold on this stuff called consciousness will eventually give rise to the respect I speak of. Perhaps the Zero Point nature of consciousness now being experimented with by respectable physicists will yield access, conscious access, to the one mind of the universe. (Theoretically, the Zero Point Field is the unifying force that underlies the potential and existence of the universe. This concept is especially interesting but also somewhat technical. For a great review of the work, see Lynne McTaggart's book *The Field*.)

Is it possible that our minds are indeed some sort of sophisticated transceiver?

Rupert Sheldrake has demonstrated what he calls the M-Field. People who are taught Morse code in a dedicated room experience both an easier learning curve and greater retention after previous groups have studied Morse code in the same room.[7] Is it possible that our minds are indeed some sort of sophisticated transceiver? If so, is tuning in to love and light versus greed, avarice, and anger just a matter of the station we choose to listen to?

Meditation studies have shown that when groups meditate on peace, crime rates fall.[8] New research into life after death, particularly the work by Gary E. Schwartz, Ph.D. (see his book *The Afterlife Experiments*), has yielded surprising evidence for life after death.[9] Near-death experiences have not been adequately explained by the so-called debunkers, and the data suggesting parapsychological abilities just keep increasing.

Researching Consciousness

In my lifetime, many of my associates and acquaintances have challenged the paranormal. Many scientists and sciolistic thinkers often treat this subject as totally foolish and unscientific. The so-called paranormal or psychic phenomena, the near-death experiences, the reports of reincarnation, astral projection, auras, and so on are all dumped into a bin of laughable irrelevance reported by delusional people or individuals under the influence of chemistry, including their own brain chemistry, such as is argued with near-death experiences.

Not all scientists view the extraordinary with such disdain and ignorance, however. Indeed, some of the greatest thinkers of all time, including this century, have conducted solid research and otherwise made serious scientific inquiries that have led to conclusions favoring a nonlocal mind interacting in a holographic universe via principles including thought and belief, and thereby co-creating what most call reality. It is definitely worth noting that as Lynne McTaggart points out in her book *The Intention Experiment,* science has clearly demonstrated that "[t]hought is a tangible thing with the power to affect the physical world!"[10] In a private communication with me, Ms. McTaggart added this: "We've played around with the idea for many hundreds of years that our thoughts can change the world around us. For most, though, it's an idea that has been dismissed as so much wishful thinking. But dig a little deeper—as I have been doing—and you discover extraordinary evidence to suggest that this really is possible, that our thoughts are another form of energy that impacts and influences the so-called physical."

Great books have been written in just the past decade that reveal a universe quite different from the one taught in high school physics. Charles Harper's work *Spiritual Information,* Thomas Campbell's *My Big Toe,* Fritjof Capra's book *The Web of Life,* Michael Talbot's work *The Holographic Universe,* Amit Goswami's eloquent book *Physics of the Soul,* and so many more clearly convolute the expectation of most with a new worldview that has mind inextricably connected with what we think of as matter and reality. I do not wish to slight any of the writers and scientists who are contributing to this remarkable revolution in physics, so please accept that the works just cited are but a few of the great ones now in print. (A recommended list of readings is in the back of the book.) Suffice it to say, consciousness, mind, or whatever you wish to call the quintessential you, is not local, not body, not ego, not what you might have believed in the past, but much greater than we can imagine. In a very real sense, the quintessential you is, like Plotinus, ineffable. The bottom line is this: phenomena and miracles happen!

Unexplainable Events

For my part, I have always known as much. As a small boy I had experiences that cannot be explained other than by some paranormal means. I somehow noetically knew things without knowing how I knew. I was able to locate lost objects, identify disturbances around people, and so on. In fact, I have found in my years of traveling and lecturing that most young people have similar experiences but learn to shut them down because of the ridicule that comes in the name of "imagination." It's all in your imagination, as if this were itself a bad thing.

As a teenager, I experienced something that I can never forget. Let me share that story with you, for part of making your choice about whatever life you wish to have is influenced by your view of this world and any possible afterlife.

One evening with my date, a beautiful young woman named Connie Bennet, I set out to pick up some money due to me before going to a dance. We were driving in a 1957 Oldsmobile on the outskirts of the small town of Woods Cross, and I suddenly began to tease Connie that we were running out of gas. It was very dark, and I stepped on the gas and then let off quickly, thereby causing the car to jerk and lunge. We were approaching several sets of rail-road tracks, and as we climbed up onto one, the car engine died. As if on cue, signal arms descended and lights began to flash. To my left I could see the headlight of the train engine bearing down on us. It seemed to be coming very fast so when Connie asked if we should get out of the car, the only thing I could think of was Connie stumbling and the car being dragged over her, so I said, "No, let me try and start the car." I turned the key, realizing the engine was flooded, and held the gas to the floor while I did so, for the 1957 Oldsmobile we were in had a Carter carburetor, which meant that when flooded, the gas pedal was to be down while the engine was started.

Connie had her hand on my leg while I frantically tried to start the engine. The next thing I knew, though, was not Connie asking for me, because I was not in the car. To be absolutely clear, I *was* in the car when the train smashed into us and *not* there when Connie was being freed.

As Connie was cut from the wreckage, and this took some time, she asked about me. The driver's side of the automobile had been crushed under the cattle guard before the car was spun and dragged down the tracks. As a result, the driver's side was only three feet high or so. As it turned out, the train consisted of approximately 100 cars and was traveling at about 100 miles per hour. I know this because of the ensuing court case, for Connie was injured and for years wore a neck brace.

The first thing I knew after the train hit us was that I was standing alone in a field alongside the railroad tracks, perhaps 50 yards from many emergency vehicles, all with their lights flashing. Several automobiles were backed up behind the now-stopped train. Some time had clearly elapsed, because Connie was not still being extracted from the car. No, she was in an ambulance, about to leave for the hospital. My first thoughts were about her, so I ran to the emergency vehicles, where I was questioned. I was taken to Connie as soon as those in charge learned that I had been driving the car.

What I have just shared with you is not possible—but it happened. My mother suggested a few weeks later that perhaps I was a walk-in, insisting that I had changed. (A walk-in is thought by some to occur when a spirit of a being chooses to leave and another spirit steps in). I didn't even know what a walk-in was at that time; what I did know was guilt for Connie's suffering. I tried to shut out the whole experience, and to some extent was quite successful for many years. However, the universe had different plans for me, and one day decided to bring it all back.

Do Miracles Have Meanings?

Miraculous events, unexplainable phenomena—one thing I have learned is that we have all experienced them at some time or another, and some people have experienced many. At the time, the event can be huge, but for most of us it doesn't take long before the memory is relegated to the back corners of our mind, and lots of us simply forget them totally. It is as though we make a conscious choice to disregard that which cannot be explained. I feel that this is a mistake. In fact, I believe that these events can hold important clues for us with regards to the *purpose* for our lives.

It took many such events for me before I started paying attention to them. I cover a lot of these in my book *What Does That Mean?*, along with the process I went through to connect the dots in my life. My hope with this particular book was that readers would use many of the same techniques to uncover deeper meaning to their own lives.

As I said earlier, though, while we have these experiences, most of us just forget them. By speaking about them, however, I have been fortunate to hear from many readers about their own fantastic stories.

One evening while sharing the train-accident story with George Noory on his popular Coast to Coast AM radio show, a listener sent me this e-mail: "I am listening to you on C2C, and must tell you another story like yours: In 1995, my roommate's cousins were in a car wreck. The cousin had her 2 small kids, ages 7 and 9, and her sister's son with her in the car when it became airborne. Mom and daughters were catapulted into a huge tree, killing them instantly. The sister's son, age 7, however, was not injured. He went to the next house to get help. When asked what happened, he said, 'Big hands reached in and lifted me out and set me beside the road.'"

Here's another: "Greetings . . . I had an experience like yours back in the early 1980s on my way back from work on I-95 in South Florida. I ran out of gas with an 18-wheeler tailgating me. I closed my eyes and prayed for God to 'be with me,' sure of my impending doom. The next thing I know I am safely on my exit ramp as the truck drove by. It had to have teleported *through* me and my '76 Mercury Comet."

I have received many, many more stories of life-changing miracles since *What Does That Mean?* was published. If you have one, I invite you to write me and share your story. You can do so by sending an e-mail to **eldon@eldontaylor.com**.

Connecting the Dots

There is a statement that had long puzzled me: Live into yourself. *What on earth could that mean?* I used to wonder. Today I have a fuller understanding of what it means, and it has become one of my favorite sayings. It is very easy to dismiss our own experiences. Everyone I have spoken to has at some time in their life had an experience that defied our so-called traditional means of understanding. Call it a miracle, call it an anomaly, call it something we are simply yet to work out and understand—that is of no consequence to the real issue at hand, which is: what did the experience tell you? When we examine our experiences, we see stories emerge. Repeated themes present errors, ambitions, weaknesses, and strengths. Perhaps when we begin to think that we are not worthy, some unexplained intervention in our lives occurs. What does that suggest to us? Perhaps when we give up faith, something takes place to rekindle our belief. Why these things happen is relative and relevant to the person they happen to. It is a part of a larger narrative.

When we ignore or dismiss the unexplained in our lives, we close the book on our story. How on earth are we ever to know ourselves if we won't even pay attention to our own story? Living into ourselves insists that we accept our experiences as our story and listen and learn from that story, for it is the most important story of our life!

Look closely at your own life. What unexplainable events have happened to you? Although in the beginning you may think that there have not been any such situations, as you open yourself up to them, and with some thought and time, you will find more and more.

I believe that it is by paying attention to the miracles in your life that you can find personal answers to the questions *Why am I here?* and *What am I supposed to be doing?* When you are in the flow, you live with a sense of satisfaction. Even when things are hard, you rest well, knowing that you are being true to yourself and doing what is right for you.

The Expansive Mind

My point here is simple: mind is not a local event. Whatever mind is, we share it in many ways. Consciousness is not understood, let alone properly defined. The rectorship of life, whatever life is, includes events and experiences that defy normal explanations and thus become paranormal. We are all much more than just a physical body with an organic brain sending signals along neural pathways like some sophisticated piece of machinery. Consciousness connects all of us in some manner or another, and it would appear to survive. As I once wrote in *The Little Black Book,* when we die we do not take with us our fancy cars, our houses, our awards and diplomas, and so forth. No, the only thing that survives with us is our relationships.[11]

◉◉◉◉◉◉◉

CHAPTER 13

THE SUBTRACTION GAME

*"An error doesn't become a mistake
until you refuse to correct it."*

— O. A. BATTISTA

It is a natural human characteristic to desire a certain quality of life. As such, it is fair to ask, *What is quality of life?* Most, when thoughtful, consider quality of life to include at least the following three characteristics: 1) absence of fear, 2) loving relationships (support), and 3) fulfillment of necessities (food, water, shelter, and health care). Contrast these desired characteristics with the typical self-image, and a couple of issues immediately emerge. First among them is the fear generated within ourselves over the risk of exposure or rejection. Next, the distance generated between people when genuine and total honesty is not forthcoming in a relationship. Third is concern over the most basic needs in life due to an absence of self-confidence—confidence in the ability to provide, especially into retirement. The common denominator in all of this is obvious—fear.

What is fear but an emotional assumption that we lack the ability to negotiate a desired quality of life? When cast in the light of Singer's four representations discussed earlier (actual self, ideal self, ought-to-be self, and desired self), where in the mental rehearsals of self does this fear arise? Does it root itself in any of these selves, or is it rooted in the differential between them?

The answer, in my opinion, is all of the above. Typically, our mental rehearsals do not include reconciliation of the selves, so to speak. That is, the original childhood rehearsals are perpetuated in some form or another into adulthood. We rehearse what we might have said, or how we should have responded, and these rehearsals are just as glamorous in a "Hollywood" sense of the word as they were when we were children. This glamorous perspective seeks to make heroes or heroines out of us. It is a game the famous philosopher Krishnamurti called "One-Upmanship."[1] All too often, it is a "get even or get evener" response that seeks to claim some victory, at least in our minds, that is rehearsed. Like a child, some seem tethered to the notion that their worth is fragile and best redeemed at the expense of others. In other words, if I make someone else feel inferior, then I have established my own superiority.

It is a strange world we live in when the criteria for establishing one's self-worth are based on the subtraction method. Subtract from John and Sally and Luke, and we somehow gain? The mature adult quickly recognizes the fallacy inherent in this kind of thinking. The circular nature of getting even or "getting evener" creates a world of insecurities and distortions, both in the physical and the mental. R. D. Laing has stated that the condition of the normal man is one of self-alienation.[2] Laing continues with strong words that are altogether too true, insisting that man pretends to be what he is not until he loses what he is.

The truth is that whenever we denigrate another, we subtract from ourselves. To the precise degree that we make less of another, we make less of ourselves. Further, this precedent subtracts from all of humanity's potential. Humankind's unkind tolerance for unkind deeds perpetuates only unkindness. Thus, fear itself is fed both by the acts of unkindness and by the inherit circularity of getting even.

What We Resist . . .

Here is a Taoist saying: "What we resist we become." In our resistance to being mocked, ridiculed, criticized, or in any other way treated in some undignified way, we create the very thing we desire to eliminate. We choose to "fight fire with fire," and in the end find ourselves burning away our own dignity and potential. All of this begins with our mental rehearsals, most of which arise from scenes right out of some television or theatrical presentation. Hollywood heroes and heroines of the kind who are portrayed in get-even events may make cute sitcoms, but not serious role models.

Remember our flowerpot story? Can you imagine a Hollywood production that portrayed such a thing? Have you ever made such a mental rehearsal? Think about it this way: Of the potential outcomes in the various scenarios, which one is going to make you feel good 20 years later? Which choice is going to feed your character, your esteem, and your integrity in years to come? Which will subtract from your sense of personal well-being?

> *The box many find themselves in is*
> *self-defining and confining.*

Thinking out of the box, so to speak, is the kind of thinking all of us must do if we are to get out of the box. The box many people find themselves in is self-defining and confining. The walls of the box are fear, anger, lack, and the like. Some circle the walls, pacing like trapped animals, failing to look up from their feet enough to see just how easy the walls are to step over.

> *The walls of the box are*
> *fear, anger, lack, and the like.*

The longest journey, Lao-tzu stated, begins with a single step. Recognizing the walls for exactly what they are and how they got there is the first step in freeing ourselves. Deciding to step out of the confines of "the same old, same old" is the next step. It is a new, genuine choice. It is a change in beliefs.

Belief is a powerful force. Belief makes a sugar pill a powerful medicine. Belief leads sane people to do insane things. Belief can enable or diminish the human potential. The belief that it's okay to get even, which is almost a social custom, is a destructive belief. Most of the beliefs many of us hold have been inherited, and often they are chicken-yard beliefs. Changing our beliefs may be the most empowering and most difficult aspect of personal growth. Self-limiting beliefs are exactly that—self-limiting. For years I have referred to such beliefs as "value norm anchor points," and they can truly be anchors. Merriam-Webster defines *anchor* as "something that serves to hold an object firmly." As discussed earlier, belief anchors exist everywhere. They arise from many facets of society. They can be shown in popular sayings, even seen on bumper stickers, such as "Money is the source of evil" and "Thank God it's Friday." What do these beliefs do? TGIF essentially communicates how much we hate our work week. Characterizing money as evil says, "I like evil and want it" or "I don't want it!" Think about the sayings you know and perhaps use. What do they communicate? Do they speak of abundance? Do they address your real desires? In other words, do they serve you?

If prosperity is something you seek, will you obtain it if in the back of your mind is the idea that it will corrupt you—that you will become evil? If excellence in the work place, maybe a promotion, is what you seek, will TGIF get you there?

Most people hold beliefs that are mutually exclusive. That is, they seek prosperity and believe that prosperity is evil. At some point in their lives, the conflicting beliefs challenge one another. Because this dissonance is typically unconscious, the stronger belief wins. Our beliefs are strongest if fear is attached to them. So, the "biggest" fear wins. The marvelous book and movie *Harry Potter and the Prisoner of Azkaban* portray a scene in which the only magic that can overcome evil is derived by calling upon a powerful memory of joy and love. When Harry finds that love-joy mix, he is able to dismiss the evil, but only then. This is a powerful, true-to-life metaphor. The only force stronger than fear is love. Somehow, though, the John Wayne "Fill your hand, you son of a bitch" metaphor is given more value in real life than "whatever you do unto the least of thy brethren." Why is that?

Again, it is the circularity of fear that perpetuates itself and, unfortunately, infects altogether too many people. Building self-worth, then, begins by examining both one's beliefs and one's fears.

Aspects of Love

Love is a soft word that would-be macho types could have difficulty dealing with. It is not used here in the romantic sense, but as an alternative to anger and fear. A helping deed done without an eye to reward is an act of love. A kind word is an act of love. A reassurance in time of need can be an act of love. Kindness is love.

Behind my former offices is a small waterway that handles runoff. It usually has some water in it year-round, and birds gather there early in the morning to drink. I used to find a gentleman there every morning when I got to the office before 7. He had an old automobile and dressed in old clothes—but every morning he was there with two or more loaves of bread, feeding the birds. This one man has made this small area, perhaps a quarter of an acre, a unique heaven on earth for the local birds. His kindness is an act of love, but if you met him, a rather large, rough-looking man, you might be put off by background thoughts (beliefs), and it is unlikely you would see him as the gentle man he is. The word *love* may be out of vogue for those who need to prove something, but it never is for those who know who they are.

There are three basic elements to nonromantic, unconditional love. The first may surprise you. It is quite simply awe. Children fall in love with everything. Little ones love the noise of a new toy, the motion of the wind, the majesty of a tall tree. They find awe in almost everything. Awe brings a glow to their faces and puts laughter on their lips. They can cry as though they have lost their dearest loved one when a toy breaks. Their innocence is not the lack of critical mental abilities as is so often thought. Their innocence truly sees the beauty, the joy, and the awe in so much of all that surrounds us each day. Awe is the realization that simple explanations do not begin to address the beauty of a rose, the words of a talented poet, the myriad faces that smile back at a smiling face on a busy street. Awe is the wonderment that empowers and ennobles the human spirit. Awe recognizes the miracle behind every breath we take. Awe sees the glory of creation for what it is, an unexplained event of monumental, even ineffable, stature.

Unfortunately, our chicken-yard training tends to diminish awe with explanations, so we learn about Darwinian evolution and the big bang theory, but our teachers fail to share with us that neither one is proven or fact. They are but the modern, albeit scientific, stories we tell our young people, and of course, we scoff or laugh at myths taught generations ago that told the story differently. We are not told that only DNA can create DNA and that, according to some, the original elements necessary to create DNA did not exist in the soup that was present on earth when life supposedly just appeared from nothing.[3] We are not told that the big bang theory has undergone many revisions just to avoid the old *Unmoved Mover* arguments (Aristotle's assertion that the first cause was intelligent and did not require an efficient cause outside of itself, and thus he referred to this cause as the Unmoved Mover.)

We learn many things this way, and therefore we dismiss their beauty and awe. We turn our lights on and enjoy the electric service, knowing where electricity comes from but failing to recognize that even science has never explained where electricity truly comes from. Oh, we can give an electron a name and explain most of its behavior, but electron jumps and other anomalies are simply left out of the teaching. If we don't understand it, the rule is to ignore it. So long as something can be named, then a certain familiarity is born and, further, a sense of knowing what something is by knowing what it is called. This is not elegant, nor is it a deliverance from the so-called noncritical abilities of a small child.

Awe is everywhere if we stop to sense the world around us. Love begins with a capacity for awe. Awe has many synonyms, including *humility,* which is a character asset that can be cultivated in our beliefs. The character aspects of each of us ennoble the human condition.

Another basic element in love is empathy. The trite but true saying "Unless you have walked in another man's shoes" is an outward expression of the empathy we can seek to encourage. Merriam-Webster defines *empathy* this way: "the action of understanding, being aware of, being sensitive to, and vicariously experiencing the feelings, thoughts, and experience of another . . ." or "the capacity for this."

The third element is best stated in a question: Am I attached to the outcome? Unconditional love is not attached to an outcome. Giving love to another is not an instrument of negotiation. All those times you may have heard something like "If you loved me, you would _____" may have unconsciously conditioned you to expect quid pro quo from love, but that kind of love is a quasi-contractual obligation. Unconditional love is not bargained for. When given, it is not given with an eye to indebtedness. Unconditional love is simply love—with no expectation or attachment to any outcome.

You may ask, as I once did, is it possible to give unconditional love? Is it possible to love someone—a child, for example—and not be committed to an outcome for that child? After all, parents want many things for their children. If the love is truly unconditional, then it survives even if the child leaves home and wants nothing to do with the parents. As in the biblical story of the prodigal son, the love remains. It is said that God loves us all this way, and where there may well be something God would have had us do differently, God's love never abandons us.

True self-esteem comes from what we give,
not from what we take.

In short, we build esteem by adding, not by subtracting, and we add most when we add from unconditional love. When we go to the aid of another, and do so without an eye to what we might get out of it, we add both to our worth and to the worth of humankind in general. When we give love without condition—no strings attached, so to speak—we add again both to our worth and to that of another. True self-esteem comes from what we give, not from what we take. It comes from the walk we walk, not from the things we say. True self-esteem builds character, not ego. It is, after all, the act of being who we really have been created to be. Further, our intention to give unconditionally creates a field that generates opportunities beyond the scope of selfish intentions.

Character Building

Believe it or not, new research shows that character building leads to better health. Indeed, one study presented to the American Psychological Association's 120th annual convention, under the title of "Science of Honesty," reported that the link between less lying and better health was significant.[4]

When I studied psychology, the wisdom of the time suggested that personality became fixed at a very young age and that IQ was fixed. The authorities of the era would have scoffed at the notion that the mind somehow could act upon the DNA molecule. Today we know that personality can change, IQ is *not* fixed, and the mind can influence the DNA molecule. A study reported in 2012 showed that the key to improving our lives was in changing our personalities.

Lead author of that study, Dr. Chris Boyce, from the School of Psychological Sciences at the University of Manchester, said, "We found that our personalities can and do change over time—something that was considered improbable until now—and that these personality changes are strongly related to changes in our wellbeing." He continued, "Compared with external factors, such as a pay raise, getting married or finding employment, personality change is just as likely and contributes much more to improvements in our personal wellbeing."

Dr. Boyce's concluding remarks are worthy of special attention: "Our research suggests that by focusing on who we are and how we relate to the world around us has the potential to unlock vast improvements in our wellbeing."[5]

Focusing on who we are, becoming truly mindful, considering how much of it is persona and how much is genuinely our true selves, separating the two, resolving our conflicts, emptying our long bags, neutralizing our fears, dissolving our angers, adjusting to our true worth (the unlimited potential that resides within), and accepting ourselves while we journey forward into living fully into ourselves—that is the ultimate frontier! You are both the explorer and the vehicle. The courage to really challenge yourself—well, that's what comes next, isn't it?

CHAPTER 14

⊛◈⊛◈⊛◈⊛

THE COURAGE TO CHALLENGE YOURSELF

"It is never too late to become the person you might have been."

— ATTRIBUTED TO GEORGE ELIOT

It takes a lot of courage to create real changes in your life. Not only does it require altering some beliefs and habits, but it first requires scouring yourself for what it is that you believe, how and why that belief serves you, and what you would like to replace it with. Let me flesh that all out a bit.

Beliefs that are self-destructive nevertheless serve some purpose, even if they sabotage our desired ambitions. It's not uncommon, by way of a simple example, for a person to become ill in order to avoid performing. When that happens, it is always an illness of opportunity: the opera singer terrified of performing gets a throat infection, and the ballet dancer suffers from a sprained ankle. Then, of course, there are defense strategies that kick in, as in my favorite instance, when the belief that the love of money is the root of all evil stops us from becoming successful and therefore evil.

Our emotions all too often control our thinking. We can become blinded by bias, find that our ideas exist within a framework that is false to the real world, hold mutually exclusive ideas and be unaware of it, define the world in ways that make no sense—such as enjoying the saliva in our mouths but finding it vile when it is put into a glass and we are asked to drink it—and so much more. Indeed, my book *Mind Programming* has several chapters devoted to just these sorts of mental traps, but for our purposes here, suffice it to say that change takes courage.

It is worth pointing out that we need always to be on the alert for these automatic mechanisms so that we use our noggins to think and not as hammers to pound home our opinions. Here are a couple of examples.

Emotional Investments

Sometimes I use my Facebook page to conduct little experiments. One day just before the 2012 U.S. Presidential elections, aware of the strong emotional division between liberals and conservatives, I decided to test awareness of both with a controversial post. It was about the forensic experts and the evidence they had assembled to argue that President Obama's Internet-published birth certificate was not authentic. I asked for opinions regarding the specific evidence assembled to show that the document had been altered by computer. Not one person responded to my question, but a great many responded to the post. Some were inflamed by the idea that some "birther" was out there arguing such nonsense against our sitting President, and others were quick to insist that they knew he had not been born in America.

Yet the question I asked had absolutely nothing to do with the President or his birthplace! It was solely about the document and the method used by the forensic experts examining the document. There is a difference, and when we fail to see such differences, we are blinded by our emotions—we may as well be using our heads as hammers to pound home our opinions based on our emotional investment.

Here's another example. I posted a study that found a physical difference between conservative and liberal brains that arguably predisposed certain types of information processing. The study suggested that conservatives were more likely to see danger than liberals were. Further, conservatives would be more concerned with their neighbors and their country, whereas liberals would be more interested in global initiatives. I did not write this study and had nothing to do with it; I only posted it. The post was a link to the article that appeared in *Science Daily,* so it could not have been mistaken for something I was saying.[1] My only comment was that this study was interesting.

Once again, many individuals had remarks to make about the post, but few about the study. One person actually sent me a rather nasty note to inform me that she would no longer have anything to do with anything I was involved with and would tell everyone she knew to do the same—and then she "unfriended" me. This person blasted me because she took the post to be my opinion rather than simply reading the study as one conducted by other researchers and then commenting on their methods.

In my view, it is often as if our emotional investments put us in a trance.

Living in a Trance

Have you given any thought to the idea of living in a trance, perhaps to the degree of the movie *The Matrix,* suggesting that some of us may well be living in a trance within a trance. In fact, there are all sorts of trancelike conditions that affect us all. Normally, when you think of trance, your thoughts might turn to altered states of awareness, such as those caught in some science-fiction spell or a person on a stage behaving like a chicken when commanded to do so by the stage hypnotist. Indeed, Merriam-Webster defines *trance* as:

1. stupor, daze
2. a sleeplike state (as of deep hypnosis) usually characterized by partly suspended animation with diminished or absent sensory and motor activity
3. a state of profound abstraction or absorption

Interestingly, the state of normal consciousness is not included in that definition. Is it possible to be in a trance and walk around thinking you are not? What would that be like, and how would you know?

If we look again at the third definition, perhaps we can build a case for normal trancelike states. Think of it this way: How many times have you found yourself so totally absorbed in your thinking that you paid no attention to your driving, only to snap out of it when your exit or some other immediate issue presented itself to you? How many times have you sat down in front of the television and became so absorbed that you didn't hear another person in the room addressing you? How many times have you found yourself off in some abstraction, imagining or daydreaming as you did when you were a child, ignorant of what was going on around you? Or for that matter, how many times have you been listening to some lecture or speaker and found your thoughts wandering off so that you didn't really hear what was said? Or how many times has your emotional investment blinded you to the logic of a position or the facts before you?

You can also think about your normal waking life in terms of brain-wave activity. Remember, in normal consciousness our predominant brain-wave activity is called beta, typically between 15 and 30 cycles per second. When we slip into an altered state of consciousness, such as hypnosis, our brain-wave activity slows to alpha, which is between 8 and 14 cycles per second. Now, if we are deep hypnotic subjects or trained meditators, brain-wave activity can slow even more to theta, which is between 4 and 8 cycles per second. When we dream, our brain-wave activity moves into the alpha range. When we first awake and remember a dream clearly, we are coming up from theta/alpha, but when we slip our feet out of bed and the dream vanishes, we have moved into beta. (For more information on hypnosis, see my book *Self-Hypnosis and Subliminal Technology*.) It's also worth noting that when we fall asleep and as we wake up, we go through twilight stages—what are technically called hypnagogic and hypnopompic states of consciousness. In other words, every day we go in and out of all these trances.

Yet there is another trance—and in my view, it is the most important to understand. That is the trance of the hive, or hive consciousness. What do I mean by that?

Hive Consciousness

We live in a 24/7 age of information, and information rules. Understand *that!* The media informs us of what is new, what is selling, and what is happening, and it even biases our likes and dislikes. The media engineers our ambitions, our habits, and our wants. The media has such control over us that we tend to live under the power of a "media-ocracy." As I pointed out in *Mind Programming,* hundreds of billions of dollars have been spent by neuromarketers to determine how our psychology is plumbed, what motivates us, what stimulates us, and what works to meet our threshold of arousal and appeals to our basic drives while instilling just enough uncertainty or fear that it's easy to feel compelled to act. And don't think that you can fix this just by turning off the television. You are still being subjected to the opinions and ideas of those around you—and they too have been programmed.

Being in a trancelike state might well be the norm for many human beings—experiencing mass hypnosis of sorts, being manipulated to consume, and having our thinking managed by others. All the while, we pretend to be ourselves. We put on a suit and wear our suit behavior. We change into our casual attire and wear our relaxed behavior. We put on our grubbiest clothing, and our behavior changes yet again. We are master chameleons—changing our actions according to our environment, exhibiting trained behavior according to what we wear, and having instant thoughts in the form of sound bites. We have imagined conversations following many of our new or unfamiliar interactions, rehearsal after rehearsal—but what are we rehearsing? Ourselves? Our authentic selves? I think not.

We all experience many interesting thought patterns that typically go unnoticed. Why? Because we tend to ignore or take for granted the conversations that go on in our heads. We all have patterns that have been with us most of our lives. They reside in our subconscious or unconscious (again, I use those terms in this context as synonyms). We rarely subject ourselves to genuine scrutiny—a real self-inquiry, an honest investigation and evaluation of who we are. Oh, we may blame ourselves, we may feel guilt, we may think we're stupid, and so forth, but those negative impressions are usually the result of something someone else has said or done to us and are themselves a part of the trance. In other words, only in our honest, authentic self can we escape the trance! Let me repeat that: *only in our authentic self are we free of the trance*—for we are otherwise in a stupor, believing ourselves to be something that we are not.

Look for Inconsistencies

One way to discover the influence of sound-bite reasoning is to search your mind for inconsistencies, for what professionals refer to as cognitive dissonance. For example, if you listen to much of the popular logic bandied about these days, you quickly discover that somehow it's not the time to be driving around in an expensive automobile, yet most people want one. The logic goes like this: Successful people represent the rich, the other one percent, who should be taxed heavily because, after all, many of them are dishonest. They're the Wall Street and banker crowd, the Bain Capital types, and the like.

Allow me to illustrate this point from my own experience. I left home at a very young age. I had the clothes on my back and a trusty Ronson lighter that was my light and heat at night. I moved into a gutted-out milk truck that was to be converted into a camper of sorts. No heat, no lights, no bathroom. I did have a job, and so while I attended high school, I worked to support myself, and in time I could afford a room with a bath. Many people in my life have been incontrovertibly indispensable to my success, but they all worked just as hard as I do, and no one else did it for any of us. It was our risk.

Here's the point. If you consider the successful to be greedy or evil or inherently overpaid for what they do, and therefore subject to a different set of rules, such as ever heavier tax burdens, then why would you want to work long and hard to be successful? In short, if prosperity is your dream, how can you condemn it on one hand and seek it on another? Instead of thinking about that person in the Bugatti, Aston Martin, Lamborghini, or Ferrari as a fat cat who probably did something unethical or illegal, wouldn't it make more sense to think about him or her in these terms: *Wow—great for you. That's for me, too!*

Consistency in our beliefs is critical, because there is no such thing as a belief that is not connected in some way to the vast web that is all of our beliefs. If money is the root of all evil in your belief system, then you will push yourself away from it when it approaches and wonder why your best efforts all seem to fail. That is not just dissonant; it is self-sabotage!

Our purpose here is not to pursue the many tricks, devices, manipulations, and conditionings that have produced our programming and continue to do so. Rather, it is to make you aware of them, for to wake up presupposes that somehow the discovery is made that, in even the smallest of ways, we are asleep. That said, it would be remiss of me not to address some of the mechanical limitations that predetermine how we react to information or process it and therefore allow dissonant beliefs to coexist.

Thought Monitoring

The first mechanical limitation that occurs to me is the way in which we are hardwired when it comes to analytical information processing. For example, analogously, there are different circuits for empathic response and analytical processing. What does that mean? Think of it this way. If I am glazed over in my emotional reaction to some sound bite, image, or idea, then my analytical process fails to operate. Instead of applying reason to arguments made by the one we feel empathy for, the one whom we trust or identify as our hero or heroine, we continue to rely on our emotions. If someone challenges our reasons at that point, we typically fail to be reasonable. We may respond with arguments, but if they fail, we will almost certainly become enraged. Why? Because we know we're right, and our feelings assure us of that.

There are many other mechanical aspects about being human that govern us just as surely as there are operating limitations to our many machines. It is ignorant to think otherwise, not that they must operate, but that in order for us to override them we must be aware that they are there.

You may remember, as mentioned earlier, the episode of *Britain's Got Talent* when singer Susan Boyle appeared. Here was a disheveled spinster in apparel circa 1950 making her worldwide debut. The audience laughed, jeered, rolled their eyes, and more. Yet when she opened her mouth and began to sing, the most mellifluous sound emerged. The audience and the judges were taken aback—but why? What makes us think that a singer should look a certain way?

Monitoring our thoughts, learning who we really are, is pretty straightforward and does not require the genius of a rocket scientist. That said, it does require the persistence of the most tenacious creature you can imagine. Thought monitoring is essential if you're ever going to truly understand yourself or become fully mindful. So, when I run into those thought patterns that are not in my best interest, I pay attention. I sometimes find myself having what I refer to as the "Krispy Kreme" conversations. This label arises as the result of a lecture I once attended when the facilitator, Dr. Brian King, spoke of habits and how the nucleus accumbens asserts, or inserts, itself. The story goes like this:

One day, King decided to lose some weight. Since he loved Krispy Kreme doughnuts so much, he concluded that he could easily lose the pounds if he avoided his favorite treat. Conveniently, he had just moved, and the nearest Krispy Kreme was about five miles down the interstate, so he would simply not get on the interstate. Problem solved.

This strategy worked for the first month or so, but the day came when he needed to travel out of town. Once he was on the interstate, the first thing that came to his mind was Krispy Kreme. Then he began a dialogue in his head that went something like this:

> *Krispy Kreme. I could stop for one doughnut.*
> *No, you would never get just one.*
> *Well, I was going to stop for coffee somewhere anyway, so why not there?*
> *Because you wouldn't just get coffee, and you know it.*

Yeah, but I have been good for months now; I deserve a doughnut as a reward.

You know all about habits and addictions. Listen to yourself.

It's not an addiction if I can avoid them as I have for as long as I have.

Don't kid yourself.

One doughnut—what's the real harm?

This internal conversation continued until King realized that he was parking his car in the Krispy Kreme parking lot.

I'm sure you are familiar with this kind of experience as well. For me, when this form of dialogue begins, I think, *Here goes some of that Krispy Kreme nonsense,* and turn off the switch. But turning it off is not always easy, and if you're to be truly successful, you almost always must dig down inside to really understand yourself, your motives, your fears, and your mechanism. Some of us are unwilling to make the effort necessary to succeed, and yet continue to go through the motions, implying that we are trying. Unfortunately, this form of trying is like changing clothes. We may behave somewhat differently, but we are still the same person, albeit often hiding from ourselves in some form of blissful trance.

Being Blissed

Not long ago I watched a TV series called *V* about an advanced alien species that invades Earth offering peace but intending quite the contrary. Their demeanor and propaganda is so good that earthlings accept their offerings and every word in absolute bliss, without question, consideration, or any intelligent enquiry. Those folks, who were thrilled to be programmed by the invaders, were referred to as being "blissed." Many people today live in a state of self-alienation and yet are unaware of it—they are blissed, if you will.

Years ago I picked up what turned out to be two of the most influential books I've read in my life. They continue to hold my attention, because they speak to the truth of our human endeavor. On one hand is the potential, and no one expressed this better than

Richard Bach in his classic *Jonathan Livingston Seagull*.[2] On the other end of the continuum, as I discussed earlier, is the work of British psychiatrist R. D. Laing and his book *The Politics of Experience,* in which he discusses the condition of alienation. The way I see it, self-growth is only possible when you allow for the possibility that you might be wrong, when you learn to question yourself from every direction, when you stop accepting the limiting norms that society attempts to place on you—and instead strive for the seemingly impossible. Then, and only then, can you walk the path of Jonathan Livingston Seagull and break through the traps that society has placed you in and find your highest, truest self.

I encourage you to begin the journey inward. Discover yourself, and learn to love all of you. In the process, I think you will find it possible to embrace all of life with a renewed vitality and put on the clothes of the genuine, authentic you!

CHAPTER 15

◦◈◦◈◦◈◦

BREAKING THE TRANCE

"Each of us is great insofar as we perceive and act on the infinite possibilities which lie undiscovered and unrecognized about us."

— JAMES HARVEY ROBINSON

There are two questions I often hear: "Why am I here?" and "Is it too late for me?" The first has to do with purpose. For me, I believe our collective and individual purpose is service. The second has to do with guilt, fear, and even aging. Despite the many varieties in which I hear this question, it generally can be stated this way: "I think it's too late for me, and I don't deserve the best."

Your purpose is service and life is a journey, not a destination.

Sometimes the "too late" has to do with age, and sometimes with actions in life. I will tell you the same thing all sacred documents say: "It's never too late while you still draw breath." As long as you breathe, you are in motion. The entire universe is in motion, expanding and contracting—not all that different from your lungs. Without motion there is atrophy and stagnation or entropy and eventually singularity. When we do leave this plane, the moment we die nothing changes but breath. For a time, cells continue to divide, multiply, and otherwise carry on in their local communities just as they did during what we call life. What's stopped is breath.

Thoughts are in motion. Our stream of consciousness, inner talk, is in motion. Our thoughts create and communicate. Even when physically unable to do certain things, our mind can do the doing. Research has shown how prayer from a stranger at great distance can heal. It is never too late!

Once, however, I also held the notion that it was too late for me. My awakening was slow. For a long time, I refused to take a long serious look at myself. I ran from my own emotional pain and hid behind money, power, anger, hostility, and false pride. But one day I couldn't hide any longer. Little by little, the layers were peeled away until I was forced to seek my true self. I had lots of help along the way, and I guarantee that you will, too, if you choose to make the journey that seems to know no end and leads over and over only to that question, "How high is up?" The Universe will provide you with rewards and help, as it did me, because that is simply how the Universe works. Dr. Wayne W. Dyer, in his excellent work *The Power of Intention,* puts it this way: "[I]ntention is not something *you do,* but rather a force that exists in the universe as an invisible field of energy!" He continues, quoting Carlos Castaneda's work *The Active Side of Infinity:* "Intent is a force that exists in the universe. When . . . (those who live off the Source) beckon intent, it comes to them and sets up the path for attainment . . ."

You are not your mind or body—you are spirit.

According to Dr. Dyer, you cannot know the meaning of life until you connect with the power that created you. You are not your mind or body—you are spirit. Spirit is giving and creative. Spirit is kind, loving, beautiful, expanding, abundant, and receptive. Emulating these qualities begins the connection process.

Dyer also says that each of us is a God experience walking! I read this for the first time on an airplane flight, and I began to look at everyone differently. The Divine, by whatever name you prefer, creates every human being, who is therefore a Divine experience walking. I can't tell you how many smiles, rules bent, and other help I received while I held this vision of everyone I encountered: "You are a God experience walking."

Practical Metaphysics

However, let's get back to "it's never too late." In my journey, there came a point when I hungered for more metaphysical information. I enrolled in a California university, the University of Metaphysics, and by correspondence commenced a study in metaphysical science. This was not the metaphysics of an upper-division philosophy course, as I expected; rather, it was a practical metaphysics for living. I had worked for a long time, often doubling the required number of exams in order to reach their designated bachelor's level of education in this unique field of study, when they sent me the news. I was ready to advance, but to do so I had to become an ordained minister.

This was not a strictly academic environment, and I should have recognized that, but the requirement blindsided me. Still, I knew that I was not worthy of being anyone's minister, including myself.

Weeks passed, and one Sunday afternoon while reading spiritual materials, I remembered a teaching from the school. I pulled out a binder in which I kept many notes, and the letter from the university fell upon the floor. As I picked it up, I knew immediately that I missed the lessons and all the joy and change they had brought into my life. I sat back down in my recliner and held the letter in my lap.

My thoughts put me to sleep, and soon I was dreaming. This is the dream:

The Fruit of the Tree

Once upon a time, a man looked to himself and spoke: "I desire to serve God, but my life has been full of error. The example I have set is not that of a cleric. People will only scoff and say, 'Know ye them by the fruits of their tree.' Who am I, then, to speak for or of God?"

With these words circling within his head, the troubled man lay down to rest. He spoke to God: "Your will, not mine, be done."

As he drifted into sleep, pictures began appearing that told this story:

Once there stood a tree—a tree of life that was full of fruit. The limbs bent toward the earth under the weight of the lush red cherries. The cherries danced in jubilee with the breeze that bathed their tender skins and turned their fullness and vivid color to face the Father, the Sun of the heavens.

With the dew and the rain they would polish their beauty and drink of the earth—to store within the energy and vitality of life, taken from the soil through the roots and fired with the spirit of the Sun radiating through the leaves of their parent tree.

But alas, not all of the children of the tree would mature into lush red fruit. Out of an urge to experience and learn on his own, one turned away from the Father and ignored the parental warnings. Charlie, as he was known by the others, kept his life juices warm, daring the cold, frost, and elements. He began to fill with color and mature early.

Pivoting on his base, he turned away from the Sun and took shade in the leaves. Daring to fornicate with the world, Charlie refused to release the natural pesticides within himself and took up affairs with the parasites.

Soon his delicate skin was broken, and his fruit exposed. The fragrance attracted the birds, and they too feasted on his flesh. Charlie lived off the flesh and of the world. Passion, experience, and knowledge were his prize.

Then one day the gardener came. Gently, he took from the parent the pure and ripened children, leaving only Charlie behind. Hanging alone, Charlie looked about him. The fall nights were cold and lonely. His friends, the birds, were on wing, abandoning him. His flesh had spoiled, and even the insects avoided him now. His soul hung on to his tattered body. The elements he had once faced with a thrill now threatened to snap him from the stem of life. Charlie was sad and lonely. He had learned these things: knowledge is not necessarily wisdom, experience is not

THE KINGDOM WITHIN

"I want to know God's thoughts; all else are details."

— ALBERT EINSTEIN

What if the world truly is magical? What if we were created to be co-creators with all the power to manifest miraculous lives if we but believed so? What if we were our own cheerleaders, full of encouragement and rah-rah support? A friend of mine named Terri Marie wrote a marvelous little book all about being our own cheerleaders. The book, entitled *Be the Hero of Your Own Game,* suggests that we are usually good at encouraging others but then tell ourselves all the reasons why we cannot succeed. What if we believed that we were created with every good possibility in our hands to be the very best of ourselves, to use our unique talents and abilities in ways that might astound many, to have happiness, peace, balance, and harmony every day in everything we do? What if our Father in Heaven looked upon us with the love and blessings that human parents have when they behold their newborn child and with his all-good, all-powerful, and all-knowing best offered all that he had to us?

> *What if we were created to be co-creators with all the power to manifest miraculous lives if we but believed so?*

I believe that God, or whatever term you are comfortable with for the Creator, has done just that. Remember Mark Twain's story in his book *Letters from the Earth?* The point of the story was to

hide God where humankind would never look. Hide him within man—the last place people will ever look!

Mysticism

While I was lecturing abroad, a wonderful man approached me with some questions. He had resigned his priesthood two years earlier because he felt inadequate. He recognized that he had provided help to many but was disturbed that he himself was not worthy to give good advice. His thoughts were not all pure, and besides, he too was born a sinner.

We spoke for some time. I asked him several questions. In the end, he admitted that no one could be worthy according to that which he had been taught. Like many, he had been trained to believe that the Grand Organizing Designer had created him imperfectly. He was born a sinner, here to endure with courage and faith the suffering that he would experience. Further, this very suffering was necessary for him to prove his devotion and love for God. Since he had been a Christian priest, training for 12 years as such, I asked him about some of the words of Jesus. According to Jesus, "The kingdom of heaven is within." Further, "In my Father's house are many mansions," "Why would you use my words and not do my deeds?" "All that I do, you will do and more," "If you had faith but as tiny as a mustard seed . . ."—all of these quotations in context clearly suggest that God dwells within all of us. They also suggest that Christ consciousness is what we should all seek to achieve. Indeed, Jesus states very clearly that we are all his brothers and sisters. Nowhere does Christ suggest that we are poor, pitiful creatures created to suffer. The message of Christ is love!

From here our conversation entered the domain of Christian mysticism, and this led to the "I AM" presence. "I am that I am," spoken by God to Moses. The Great I AM presence is the kingdom of heaven, or God/Christ consciousness within. (This is a study worth undertaking, but one that is beyond the scope of this work, so I suggest the *I AM Discourses* published by St. Germain Press if you wish

to pursue this further.) I was then asked, "Is this the reason that all of your affirmations on InnerTalk programs begin with 'I am'?"

My mind flashed back to a small bookstore in Reno, Nevada, where nearly 20 years before I was asked the same question. "Actually," I answered, "the research shows this is the best way to state the affirmations. I do find it interesting that it is the declarative, 'I am.'" We then spoke of prayer. The ancient texts were often interpreted incorrectly. The word *ask,* when translated correctly, should read *declare.* Declaring is creating, not petitioning. At length we had traveled around the world and examined many religious systems. We agreed, whether Christ consciousness or Buddha consciousness, whether from the Upanishads or the Bible, whether Lao-tzu or Zoroaster, all the great living religions taught *love* at their core. Suffering as some creation made imperfectly and therefore unable to avoid sin, begging for salvation and so forth, was not the teaching. No—to the contrary, the God within created all with the ability to manifest miracles, if they but had faith the size of a tiny mustard seed.

It was then that the lights went on in the mind of my new friend. "Oh, I get it. When you teach people to suffer, even indirectly, you claim suffering for them and yourself. How could I have missed that? No wonder I always felt guilty and ashamed."

This gentleman has since made some remarkable changes in his life. He still helps people, but now he empowers them to help themselves. Through forgiveness, releasing guilt and blame and therefore shame, today he teaches the unlimited power within. All of this begins by taking responsibility for everything in our own life.

Earlier I suggested an acronym for fear. Let me suggest a couple more: *False Evidence Appearing Real* and *Forget Everything And Run.* You were not created imperfectly to fear the world, or anything else for that matter. You are, as Dyer puts it, "A God experience walking."

Grace

When I suggested the forgiveness messages for our prison-inmate population, there was some concern. After all, forgiveness sounds very much like grace. Accepting responsibility is fine, but forgiveness? Forgiving and forgetting, or letting go—what does that mean?

I was in my hotel room one evening when my host informed me that a gentleman had just flown in from Singapore to hear my lecture. I was told that I had been an inspiration to his work, and he wanted to meet me. The arrangement was made, and I met Dr. Mel Gill, a wonderful man with a terrific sense of humor. Dr. Gill had lost an arm and loved to joke about it. He used for empowerment what many would consider a handicap. He gave me a copy of his book *Uncommon Sense,* which I read that evening. In it, I found a chapter entitled "Forgiving or Forgetting." Mel used a marvelous metaphor that adds to our understanding of forgiveness power. When you forgive, "Who are you giving to but yourself. . . . Forgetting when split into two words (equals) 'for getting.' What are you getting in response to forgiving other people? Well, you are getting freedom."

The great I AM presence has already forgiven you, for as *A Course in Miracles*[1] points out, the real you, the Christ consciousness that is your quintessential self, is and has always been perfect, just as it was created. All you must do is accept that truth, and everything changes. Or, as in the parable of the prodigal son, return (recognize) to the Father and His house, and all is forgiven.

Life is a schooling process. Mistakes are teaching lessons. Remembering that and who you really are is awakening. There is a story about the Buddha that illustrates this point. It seems the Buddha was walking one day when he met a fellow traveler on the path. The traveler fell down at the feet of Buddha and proclaimed, "You must be God."

The Buddha answered, "No, I'm not God."

The traveler insisted, "Then you must be a demigod!"

Again the Buddha responded, "No, please get up. I'm not God or a demigod."

The traveler, confused, then asked, "Okay, tell me, what are you?"

The Buddha replied, "Only awake."

This story always reminds me of the glorious book *Letters to Strongheart*. Strongheart was among the first animal movie stars. A German shepherd, Strongheart, played the first real dog hero. When he passed over, his handler, J. Allen Boone, wrote a book that expressed imaginary letters to Strongheart with their replies from the other side. In one of these letters Strongheart states, as I recall, "What a hideous sight to behold faces as incomplete as minds."

Trying Is Not Doing

Mel Gill has identified 12 ways that people use to escape accountability in his book *Uncommon Sense*. In statements they are expressed this way:

1. I'll try.
2. If _____ then _____!
3. I forgot!
4. It's not my fault.
5. I had no choice.
6. I can't.
7. I had no control.
8. I'll wait and see.
9. I don't know!
10. It's not my job.
11. That's just the way I am.
12. Nobody told me.

Those statements are all excuses. Trying is not doing. Conditional acts are waiting, not acting. Forgetting simply says it wasn't important enough for me to write down or remember.

"Not my fault" is another way of blaming and escaping personal responsibility. No choice? What does that mean? Can't? Only if you believe you can't. The bottom line is this: You do have the power and the ability.

You Do Deserve!

Within you is an absolutely awesome potential. You deserve, and you are worthy. Your life begins anew each moment. It is never too late, and it is always right to pursue your highest potential. It is all a matter of changing some old views. Perhaps, as with me, some tool like InnerTalk aids you in getting rid of those old, negative self-beliefs. Whatever your path and your tool, you are a miracle, and you do deserve happiness. You are here to learn—not to suffer. You are a gift from the Divine, and you were not created deficiently. There is nothing for you to feel shame over. Shame is a tool of guilt. It can be used to control you and force you to deny your real higher self. What you've done in the past is a lesson, and when you understand that, accept and forgive yourself and all others, commit to your very best—all else is taken care of for you. The gifts have been given; they are there for you to accept. Again, you absolutely do have the power and ability to manifest peace, balance, and harmony in your life. You absolutely do have the power and the ability if you but believe.

Each of us is but one drop
in the proverbial sea of being.

Panentheists (process theology, also known as panentheism) use a metaphor or analogy when they speak of humankind and Creator. Just as each of the cells in your body is conscious in some way, your love and consciousness of them heal and protect all of you. You and I and all of us are analogously cells in the body of the Creator. Each of us is but one drop in the proverbial sea of being. Our Creator is conscious and loving of all of us; we need only to be conscious and loving to share in the co-creative powers endowed upon us by the act of creation. Eliminate the doubt, fear, shame, guilt, and blame and accept our true birthright. Rescript the old ANTs (Automatic Negative Thoughts), replacing them with positive, loving thoughts full of acceptance and gratitude. Reach down inside now and see if this doesn't seem so familiar and so true as to be noetic—knowledge you have always known but perhaps forgot.

In the next chapter we'll take a look at what we might expect in our journey of self-empowerment—both the rewards and the disappointments—but first let me share a story with you about struggle. Personal growth or improvement involves change, and that can mean struggle. I recall a cute little book from a few years ago that stated in its title, *"Life Was Never Meant to Be a Struggle."*[2] Perhaps that is so from a certain perspective, but for most of us, struggles are how we grow. Like the proverbial steel in the mill that grows stronger during the tempering process (heating, cooling, reheating, and so on), we grow stronger from our own struggles. So, struggle does not mean bad; rather, it should equate with growth, and it does so when our lens of perception sees life's challenges in this way. Here is the story:

The Emperor Moth

There once was a scientist who beheld the glory of an emperor moth and was so totally taken by the creature that he decided to study it. For more than a year he monitored the activities of the giant moth.

One day he came upon a caterpillar ready to spin its cocoon. He gently captured the caterpillar and took it back to his lab. He watched the caterpillar build its cocoon within a glass container and enter that state of deep sleep. While in the chrysalis it changed its form, from crawling on the ground to floating in the sky.

The day came when the moth was ready to leave the cocoon. The scientist watched anxiously as the tiny head chewed its way into the light of the laboratory. The moth struggled and struggled, seemingly getting nowhere. Its body was simply too large to fit through the tiny hole in the cocoon. The moth tired and laid its head to rest on the shell of the cocoon. The scientist took it upon himself to help the tiny creature. "How could I stand here for so many hours watching this beautiful moth go through such agony and pain?" he questioned. "Where is my mercy?" he continued as he took his tweezers and scissors to cut away the cocoon. The moth fell from the cocoon badly deformed, and soon died.

Later the scientist discovered that it was precisely the cocoon-escaping struggle that pressured the fluids down into the body of the emperor moth and gave it its aerodynamic ability. The cocoon forced the fluids into the body, perfectly proportioning the moth as it pushed its way out. Cutting away the cocoon in an effort to help had only killed the moth.

Struggle does not mean bad.

There are a couple of morals to this story. Sometimes what seems like a struggle is indeed creating improvement, and sometimes what might appear as helping is only making matters worse.

In the end, it's up to each of us as individuals to make the best of our lives. For me that means happiness, which begins with self-responsibility. Remember, you may not be in charge of everything in your world, but you are definitely in charge of your inner environment.

Now, as I promised, let's look again at change—the process of change.

CHAPTER 17

◦◉◦◈◦◉◦

CHANGE

*"All that is necessary for the triumph of
evil is that good men do nothing."*

— EDMUND BURKE

Change is perhaps the most sought-after goal in life. If we but had more money, more education, and less compulsion; if we could lose weight, stop smoking, be more popular, have more friends, and so forth, life would be perfect. Change is also perhaps the most frightening experience we can undertake. It means giving up something—some belief, some habit, some pattern, some *something*. Change from the inside out can also mean great risk.

Genuine change often means letting go of acquaintances who hold different beliefs—like our bad-luck fortune-cookie carriers. Remember, as we discussed earlier, these are the folks who build their social economy by choosing to share the worst in life, almost competing with each other for who is less fortunate. It isn't so much that we let go of them as they abandon us, for we no longer provide a sanctuary safe for "cookie" sharing. There are also plenty of naysayers. Like the smart chickens in the chicken house, they will tell you that all this is nonsense. Some may even attack you with such words as *hoax* and *fraud*. Like most attacks, they are designed to produce feelings of insecurity, doubt, even stupidity. One book out there suggests that self-help efforts generally rob people of their money and their esteem. The book is entitled *Sham: How the Self-Help Movement Made America Helpless* by Steve Salerno. I heard him tell of a sales event he attended with salesmen all from the same company. He criticized the motivational speaker on the grounds that in the beginning of the presentation the speaker told everyone in the audience that each could be the number one salesperson in the coming year. Such was a logical absurdity, he asserted, for how could they all be number one in the same company? Stop and think about it for a minute. Do you really think either the salespeople or the motivator took this statement to mean anything other than each of the individuals in the room had the ability to be number one? I don't. Indeed, I have been guilty of far worse, at least on the surface, by stating that we can win at everything!

We Can Win at Everything

Now you might say, "How is it possible to win at everything?" The answer is simple, but it is also involved in the definitions attached to winning and losing. Let me get this point straight, right from the beginning. We only lose when we let ourselves down! We can only win, in the real sense of winning, when we do our very best! Our very best requires commitment, courage, dedication, singleness of purpose or focus, and more. These attributes are fundamentally known as character.

My late friend Coach Phil Porter said, "The basis of winning is character." Phil was a ninth dan black belt in martial arts, a retired Air Force major, and the coach of many Olympic athletes. He added: "Character is simply a combination of all the virtues which have been the basis of American life."

Character is a hallmark of great champions. Character is developed. Character requires an earnest effort to be, to live, to think, and to act according to a code of conduct that dictates honesty and integrity in all things. No higher act of honesty exists than that which is necessary in order to stand back and say, "I know I did my very best!" Self-honesty can be one of the most difficult characteristics, and yet the most rewarding, a person can ever develop. The words attributed to Pythagoras ring as true today as ever:

"Above all else, know thyself!"

Words and truisms can be interesting. When I was very young, the words "all men are created equal" disturbed me. What on earth did it really mean? It was obvious to any child that all men were indeed not created equal. Adults who truly wished to settle my concern over this foolish matter gave me many answers. Their typical answer went something like, "In the eyes of God, all men are equal."

Taking Pride

Although this answer did provide some comfort, it nevertheless failed to register at every level of my being as "true." Then one day the answer was put to me another way. It went something like this: Imagine a rocket scientist who after much work launches an interstellar voyager. Imagine the pride he feels in the accomplishment. Now imagine a so-called menial laborer. On his hands and knees for endless hours, he scrubs and polishes a floor. He has worked so hard and with so much pride that he has scrubbed his knuckles raw. Now he stands back and beholds his labors. The floor absolutely glistens—every square inch of it. It never looked this good even when it was new. Now, I was further instructed, which man senses the most pride, the rocket scientist or the floor scrubber?

Even at a young age, I recognized that questions such as this one were obvious. If both men did their absolute very best and knew it, putting their whole heart, mind, and soul into their work, their pride of accomplishment would be equal. To the degree that they compromised their very best, to that precise degree their sense of accomplishment would be diminished.

Risking Change

In this day and age, change can also mean risking reputation and even our livelihoods. Is it unscientific to include the spiritual component in science? I don't think so. Again I hark back to a word of William James: *pragmatic*. Is science capable of investigating pragmatic outcomes? The answer is clearly yes.

I have experienced personal attacks for some of my work and know firsthand that when we stand outside the established norm (establishment), we may find ourselves standing alone, at least for a while. I am also fortunate to know many who stood with me and supported my work, even in the darkest hours. Today the technology and methods I have discussed for changing a person's inner beliefs, known now as InnerTalk, have been demonstrated effective in dozens of studies. Today the mind-body-spirit connection is so well established that denying it is absurd. Still, whenever individuals ask me to recommend a health-care professional who will treat them holistically rather than mechanically, I remember just how short in supply these professionals are, and then I think of Dr. Cristian Enescu.

Dr. Enescu is a prominent neurologist in New Jersey whom I have the great pleasure of knowing. He was gracious enough to write the Foreword to this book and has used many of the techniques in it to improve his life and that of his patients. Rather than tell you about him, I will let his own words, shared with my office in an interview, tell his own story. My wife, Ravinder, wrote the introduction and conducted the interview.

Dr. Cristian Enescu

For several years now, Dr. Enescu has been sharing InnerTalk with his patients and periodically would call us to share some of his amazing stories. We are thrilled that he managed to find time in his busy schedule to work on this interview with us.

Why did you choose to become a doctor?
Mathematics was my best subject in high school, and I had thought that I would become a mathematician or engineer. However, during my last year of high school, an "inner voice" was telling me that I should choose a career in which I could "help" people. It was because of this "inner voice" that I started pursuing medicine as a career.

Where did you get your training?

I graduated with honors from medical school in Bucharest, Romania, in 1983. Six years later I moved to Greece for just under a year, where I worked as a researcher. In 1990 I moved to the United States, and after working as a research associate in the neurology department at the City of Hope Medical Center in California, I entered an internship program at Brookdale University Medical Center in Brooklyn, New York. I then went on to do my neurology training at St. Vincent's Hospital in Manhattan.

Why did you become a neurologist?

During my year in Greece, I had the privilege of meeting a prominent Greek neurologist, Spyros Skarpalezos. We spent a great deal of time discussing neurology. Then during my first year as an intern, I met another neurologist, Miran Salgado, who explained to me the spiritual aspect of neurology. You see, neurology deals directly with the brain, the brain and the mind are inseparable, and the mind plays an important role in all healing. So, while as a doctor I could help people, as a neurologist I could maybe discover how my patients could use their own minds to help in their own healings. Neurology allows me not only to understand how my patient's brain is functioning, but it also gives me the opportunity to study and experiment with my own brain.

How did you first hear about InnerTalk?

During my first year as an intern, my life was busy—too busy! I needed to find ways to relax and to speed up my own recovery process so that I could function better. I searched the Internet and came across InnerTalk. I was amazed by what I read. If the information were really true, then InnerTalk had to be really important for all mankind. Of course I had to try this technology for myself. The first programs I tried were *I Am Relaxed, Using Both Halves of the Brain,* and *Synchronicity.* What I found was that previously I had known nothing about relaxation. The InnerTalk programs helped me to relax more deeply and made me aware of a much greater reality. My InnerTalk programs became my personal oasis of quietude. I went on to get many more programs, and I benefited from all of them.

What were the benefits you gained from InnerTalk?

I am an avid reader and had learned about deeper states of relaxation, which lead to a heightened awareness of reality, but I had been unable to achieve this. With InnerTalk I was finally able to put into practice what I had previously only heard about. I then started exploring the more spiritual programs, such as *Opening Up to a Higher Power* and *Using the Force,* and I worked through the *Self-Hypnosis* course. However, it was the *Path to Mastership* library that truly changed my life. You see, before using InnerTalk, I was a successful doctor, but there was no depth or real meaning to my life—there was no spiritual connection. I felt that there had to be something else in this life—something was missing. Since using InnerTalk, my life has changed dramatically. I found new joy in living, and my life became a fascinating adventure, like a huge jigsaw puzzle with pieces falling into the right places one by one.

In my practice everyone noticed the change in the message I was delivering to my patients. The financial aspects of my practice, though still important, became completely eclipsed by the daily search to find ways to awaken my patients' minds. My purpose for becoming a doctor was not just to be successful but also to truly help people, and now I feel I am doing just that.

With InnerTalk I was finally able to put
into practice what I had previously
only heard about.

When and how did you start introducing your patients to InnerTalk?

I had experienced so many personal gains from using InnerTalk that I wanted to teach my patients about this wonderful tool. Of course, this is not promoted by the mainstream medical system, which wants to preserve itself. Physicians are expected to prescribe only drugs. All other alternative ways of healing are discouraged. In my case, I provide my patients the standard neurological care, and then I offer my own insights about mind healing. I had already made the observation in my own patients that those patients who were optimistic simply got better quicker and depressed patients got worse, regardless of the treatment protocols used.

Behind my desk, my patients see a large sign that reads: "Every day, in every way, I am getting better and better." During each exam, I make sure I am playing an InnerTalk program with gentle music. My patients feel more relaxed, and I explain to them the importance of being in a healing atmosphere. I then explain the importance of the mind in self-healing. The sign on my wall is there because of some work done by a French hypnotist. He found that patients who repeated this affirmation every night got physically better, while those in the control group did not experience the same gains. I tell all my patients about this research and other such studies. I then go on to explain to my patients that InnerTalk is one of the most powerful tools to access the power of their own minds. Most people have no idea how much control their subconscious minds have over their lives.

"Every day, in every way,
I am getting better and better."

There are some older people, maybe because of their mental decline, who are not as open to these ideas, so I do not go into these new ideas in much depth. However, their families invariably are interested, so I do discuss it with them. The fact is the mind is powerful, and the mind is capable of healing the body. Health care is a team effort. As the doctor I can run the test and prescribe the medicine, but the patient must take responsibility for being positive and for creating his or her own health. I teach all my patients how to use guided imagery to picture themselves well. This technique is cheap, has no side effects, and is incredibly powerful.

With everything I teach my patients I explain the importance of being consistent and patient. Some of my patients tell me that they will try these new techniques, and I tell them not to "try" but to "do." Some of my patients want to know exactly how quickly they will see the results of these techniques. I tell them that it all depends on how much effort they put into it. Not that playing InnerTalk programs takes effort, as you simply play it in the background. But you do need to put the program in your player and turn it on! I recommend that they use the nature format at night while they sleep and the music as much as possible during the day.

I should tell you, too, as I tell all of my patients, that I have no financial incentive to tell people about InnerTalk. I do not do it for money—I do it because I believe in InnerTalk and its ability to access the power of the mind.

How responsive were your patients to these new ideas?

Some patients are very responsive to these ideas. They put into practice all I have taught them, and they get better. When they want to thank me for the benefits they have realized, I have to explain to them that the merits go to them. It is the power of their own minds that has led to their health improvements.

In some instances, patients may be afraid even to own up to the power of the mind. They simply do not want to deal with the possibility that they may be able to heal themselves. To acknowledge that is to acknowledge that maybe they created the sickness in the first place. You have to be honest with yourself before you can access the power of your own mind. In these instances I tell my patients to watch for the signs. The fact is, we all encounter instances when what we expected to happen does in fact happen. If we expect the worst, we often receive just that. If we expect the best, then that is often what we get. I will also suggest some books or movies that may help them to become more open to the ideas I am trying to teach them.

For most people, life is like going to the theater where they are merely spectators. When you learn meditation, you will find that you are a part of the movie and that you have more control over how your story unfolds. I believe that meditation and spiritual awareness can help all of us live much more fulfilling lives. I also emphasize that it is one thing to read about spirituality and meditation and quite another to actually experience it for yourself. I tell my patients not just to talk about it but also to actually go and do it. This way they can become part of the action themselves.

However, I do have to respect my patients' time. Some people simply are not ready for such radical thinking. These patients I simply treat with "traditional" methods, and while I am able to help them, they do not see the same gains as the other patients.

You obviously see spirituality as an integral part of self-healing. How do you explain these ideas to an atheist?

Much scientific work has demonstrated the power of the mind. Many experiments in physics have shown that the outcome of experiments is dependent on the expectations of the observer. You simply cannot reject the practical role of the mind. If someone does not believe in a higher power, then I approach him or her from a very scientific point of view. The studies on the mind are reproducible and therefore totally scientific. It is therefore easy for me to change my approach from that of mysticism to hard science.

*The studies on the mind are reproducible
and therefore totally scientific.*

What advice do you have for our readers?

Don't just believe me—do it for yourself. Once you have your own proof, then no one can take it away from you.

How do your colleagues respond to your approach?

I knew that I was doing something right, so it did not matter to me what my colleagues thought. My colleagues are afraid to bring spirituality into their work. They are afraid of bringing in new ideas, as they may fail and so lose patients. Doctors are generally financially secure, and if they were to believe in InnerTalk and in the power of the mind, then they would have to change. Change means taking a risk, and generally doctors do not want to take risks with their own security. Very few doctors are open to the power of the mind. I have had a few patients who were not open to these new teachings, and some of my colleagues say that I should stop teaching it as I could lose these patients. But I am not a doctor so that I can keep patients; I am a doctor so that I can help people. The fact is, if an American president is elected with 60 percent of the popular vote, it is considered a landslide victory. If I can get 60 percent of my patients to take some responsibility for their own health, then I have been successful! As it is, my approach is not losing me any patients. On the contrary, I am doing even better than before!

Change means taking a risk.

Do you have any specific stories you can share with us?

One patient I was seeing had been suffering from migraines. Ten different doctors had given her the same medications, and they had never worked. When I saw her, I prescribed the same pills. This time they worked. She was surprised. I had to ask her if it was possible that it was not the medications she had taken but rather the other changes I had asked her to implement. I then suggested that she discontinue the medications but continue with the other practices. She is now free of migraines and free of medications. The InnerTalk programs I had her use were *Forgiving and Letting Go; Headache Relief; Healing and Releasing Emotional Pain;* and *Freedom from Fears, Doubt, Helplessness, and Hopelessness.*

Another patient came to me suffering from multiple sclerosis. I told her that in order to get better, she needed not only to continue with her medications but also to pay attention to everything else that I had taught her. She started working with *Powerful Immune, Self-Healing Is Natural, Freedom from Depression,* and *I Am Relaxed.* I think that the depression program is particularly important. Patients are often depressed and expect their condition to get worse. I believe that self-healing must start with the expectation that you can get well. This particular patient worked hard to implement all I had taught her. She tried to think positive even while she did not feel any better. Eventually it paid off. She no longer uses her cane and is optimistic about her future. She knows that she will get better, and she tells everyone this. She even went back to dancing, and the quality of her life has improved immensely. Now she tells everyone about the power of the mind!

Self-healing must start with the expectation that you can get well.

I am also seeing great results with stroke patients. One of my patients, with weakness in the left side, experienced significant improvements in his walking and speech after using the Inner-Talk programs in conjunction with his "traditional" treatment. His condition improved sooner than similar patients who had not used InnerTalk.

I get similar results with patients with Parkinson's. When they use InnerTalk while taking their medications, they get better faster, their tremors improve, and their anxiety levels are reduced.

*Basically my patients get better faster
when they use InnerTalk in addition to the
rest of their treatments, as compared
with similar patients who use only
the "traditional" treatment methods.*

Do you find the doctors or the nurses more open to the concept of the power of the mind?

Nurses are definitely more open to the power of the mind. They deal with the patients from the practical side. They see that the patients who are happier get better faster. They hear me explaining the power of the mind to my patients, and it makes sense to them.

Doctors, however, start practicing after a very long training, and they are already mentally tired and want to finally relax. Because of this, they are less inclined to embark on another type of training, a training that is totally different, the training in spirituality, even though this may be the most important training of their lives.

There is a gradually increasing pressure on the medical profession from insurance companies and the malpractice crisis. The system has become so complex and so sophisticated and is drawing all the energies toward the material aspects of their lives. As a result, physicians are less and less inclined to focus on the spiritual aspects of their lives. Also, physicians do not have a clear understanding of what meditation even is. They perceive meditation as just another way to relax, the same as having a drink by the pool with friends and family. They simply do not see the training of the mind as being important. They have no idea what they are missing.

Why do you believe meditation to be so important?

We cannot progress with spirituality without learning about meditation. Meditation is so much more than just relaxing, and it is different from praying. I was brought up as a Greek Orthodox

Christian, and they believe in praying a lot. However, I see praying as "speaking to God," whereas meditation is "listening to God." Most people simply do not want to spend time working on something that seems so ambiguous, but the rewards are there for those who do.

Which programs do you think everyone should have in his or her personal library?

I think everyone should learn the true meaning of relaxation. Once you learn this, you can turn to the deeper levels of spirituality. I would therefore start everyone with the *Deep Relaxation* collection and then follow up with titles such as *Opening Up to a Higher Power* and *Connecting with the Force*. I really like the *Platinum Plus* collection, especially *Manifesting Your Vision* and *Dream Petitioning*. I think that the *Path to Mastership* is the crown jewel in the Inner-Talk line. This should definitely be in everyone's library. It is the most powerful program and works so well for the busy lives we all now live. I also use *Energy Meditation* and *Conscious Expansion,* and I think *Hyperemperia* is a must for everyone.

Are you saying that everyone should work with the spirituality programs, regardless of what their major issues are?

Most of my patients want specific results right away, but I believe that the true solutions lie in spirituality. I therefore use a combination of programs, some that are specific to a particular problem and some that deal with spirituality. This way they can see the immediate results while they work on the long-term solution that prevents the problem from coming back. It is only by reestablishing the mind-body connection that we can prevent the problems from recurring.

Are there any other titles you think we should carry in our line?

Your library is so extensive that I can always find a program that fits my needs and my patients' needs. I do not think you need to add to the line. What we need to do is tell more people about this technology. I truly believe that InnerTalk has the capability to change human civilization. It is so powerful and so needed that I think it should be in every hospital. The doctors would be able to relax so much more, and the patients would all recover faster. There is no one who cannot benefit from InnerTalk. InnerTalk truly is the tool for self-realization, and it is the best investment you could ever make. It is the best investment I have ever made, as it has changed my family life, my patients, and my professional life. I tell everyone about InnerTalk, but I am also very aware that I can only plant the seeds. I am not responsible for the germination.

Thank you, Dr. Enescu. I am sure that, like me, all of our readers have found your interview inspiring, enlightening, and educational. I wish more doctors had your dedication to truly helping their patients. I for one would be more comfortable about going to see a doctor who lived by your philosophy.

•◉•

And here is another success story that you can learn from. This one is from DeDe Murcer Moffett, who has also made huge strides in her life using the principles in this book and the InnerTalk programs. Here is her story in her own words.

DeDe Murcer Moffett

Life indeed is a multitude of choices and illusions. In many cases, the choices we make are derived directly from our illusions. Illusions, by my definition, are unfounded thoughts and unfounded beliefs that are ungrounded in truth. Nevertheless, those illusions can be powerful motivators or, depending on the feelings they evoke, "demotivators." I can promise you, I've certainly had my share of both.

My inspiration has always been music; I was born to be an entertainer. I started singing publicly at age 13. I performed in countless shows and musicals throughout junior high and high school, winning competitions and even performing abroad in Europe. Music, for as long as I can remember, was never something I just engaged in; it was something deep inside me. It was a force with no known origin, for it has always been there. My greatest desire was to be on Broadway, to take that creativity inside me and mold it into something beautiful. I wanted the outside world to see, hear, feel, and ultimately find inspiration through my entertaining.

But my own unfounded illusions would trip me up and take me on a 24-year detour from the real me before I would ultimately wake up, stand up, and snap out of it!

The turning point came soon after I received my long-sought-after and highly anticipated vocal scholarship from Oklahoma City University, the same university attended by Broadway star Kristin Chenoweth, incidentally.

I Was a "Nobody"!

During my time in college, my deep-seated fears and illusions began telling me I couldn't compete; I was a "nobody." My illusions led me to believe that I was just average, not smart enough, not pretty enough, and definitely not talented enough. Of course, you realize that no one was actually saying these things—no one but me, of course. Each day I faced paralyzing fear and internal torment. This feeling, coupled with self-hate and self-sabotage, was quickly dimming the lights on my lifelong dream of Broadway. My feelings and thoughts of being not good enough were the powerful motivator that encouraged me to make the most regrettable choice of my life.

A year after I started down the path that I thought would lead me to the bright lights of Broadway, I quit college. My vocal professor, the "Ice Queen," as I called her, stopped me at the door. "DeDe, what are you doing? You are one of my most promising students!" But I couldn't hear her—didn't want to hear her, I suppose. I just wanted to get out, away from the fear that overshadowed my talent and corrupted my dream.

Now, as I look back with wisdom honed by experience, it never dawned on me to turn around and question the validity of those fears. It never dawned on me to just feel those fears and keep on going. No, I just wanted relief, and to me, relief meant I had to get away and forget about my dream.

What was I to do with my life now? I'm confused. I'm angry. I'm sad. I'm depressed. I'm lost.

Figuratively, I snapped my fingers. "Wait! I've got it! I'll go make money! Everyone knows having money makes you feel powerful, beautiful, accepted, and happy. And maybe, just maybe, I will finally feel like a star!"

Avoiding Pain

So that's what I did. I got myself a starring role as a sales executive, and man, did the money ever come rolling in. I had the big house, the nice car, fabulous clothes, and *status*. I had everything I just knew would make me feel everything I wanted to feel.

But dreams don't die so easily, and the DeDe I left behind, the DeDe I tried to push down and tried to ignore, was still very vibrant, alive, and "vocal," some might say outspoken. She kept calling out to me, "DeDe, hey, we can still do this. We can still live our dream. It's not too late! DeDe, damn it, wake up!"

Did she really think I could to go back there, go back to pain and discomfort? No way! Has she lost her mind? She had to be drowned out. I had to shut her up before she did the unthinkable— wake me up and cause me to look at the truth of my life. I had to do something quick!

So I outsmarted her, you see. That is when I fell in love with Mr. Cabernet Sauvignon. Big, bold, charming, and suave Mr. Cabernet! I couldn't get enough. I had to have him every single night. In fact, for the next 24 years we would stay attached at the hip, smashed cheek-to-cheek, taking the world by storm! That chatty, chatty DeDe would finally be silenced!

She did stay silent for a very long time, that is, until early 2007. It was a Friday the 13th, and my fiancé and I were at a business conference in Austin, Texas. In two months we would be in Mexico at our beautiful oceanfront wedding. The problem was that I was still very much involved with Mr. Cabernet. Due to my unwillingness to end this threesome, tensions were mounting. We were like a rubber band, stretched to its limit. Now, 13 must be my lucky number. Like I said, it was a Friday the 13th, I was born on the 13th, and I had 13 glasses of wine that night. Yes, 13! Don't try this at home—it's for professionals only! Not pretty!

Silence Is Deafening

I didn't know it, but I was about to get the wakeup call of my life. You see, the morning after my pass-out-under-the-table, act-like-a-fool, 13-glasses-of-wine drink fest, everything had changed. My fiancé had had enough. He was done talking—no more begging, no more pleading, only silence. You know the silence that is just deafening? He was done. He had let go. And like a rubber band when it's released, it hit me so hard that I was snapped completely out of my 24-year, self-made illusion. Life as I knew it was over, and so was my relationship with Mr. Cabernet. It was one of the toughest things I've ever done, but I threw him out with nothing but the cork he popped in with!

By the way, my fiancé did stick with me, and we did have that beautiful oceanfront wedding. He is the spark that ignited my "snap power" and one of the main reasons I am living my dream today!

So, yes, I know very well how choices and illusions do indeed shape our lives. The question is, can we become willing to honestly look at the illusions fueling our choices? Can we wake up to the pain that led us to medicate, sedate, and control our lives, even to the point that we're now but a fragment of who we were born to be, who we really are? Can we become willing to make a different choice, especially when it's uncomfortable and unfamiliar? It took me 24 years to wake up and stand up, but now I know the answer is a resounding yes!

Eldon Taylor's InnerTalk work has been an integral part of my life for as long as I can remember. During my sales career, I purchased many InnerTalk programs like *Ultra Enthusiasm, Extreme Confidence,* and *Visualizing for Success* until I actually became a success even while I was still an alcoholic.

True Recovery!

When I decided to let go of my chosen painkiller, the one that was killing me rather than taking away the pain, I knew I needed to walk through some incredibly uncomfortable feelings and start reprogramming my mind, body, and soul. Not an easy task, so once again I turned to Eldon's InnerTalk CDs. I purchased *Ending Self-Destructive Patterns, Overcoming Alcoholism, Manifesting Your Vision,* and *Infinitely Creative.* I committed to listening to one of these programs every day for at least one hour.

My results were astounding, nothing short of a miracle! In 2008, the anesthetized DeDe finally woke up, and she stood up and snapped back to life! She was alive. She could actually feel again.

Yes, I finally integrated my two DeDe's. My creativity and courage began to explode. My passion for singing and entertaining was back in full force. I have no illusions about some of the techniques that aided me on my path. The daily listening to Eldon's Inner-Talk programs significantly influenced my thinking and helped changed the direction of my life.

When you believe in you, when you believe you can, that's when miracles happen. I often think about the difference between that girl who drank for 24 years and this new girl today. There is really only one difference: her mind. My talents and my abilities lay within me always, just waiting for me to wake up and believe.

Since waking up, standing up, and snapping out of it, I have been experiencing some incredibly fulfilling opportunities and projects. In 2008, I created a highly successful interview-style radio show called *The Snap Out of It! Show* and then established my own radio network, the Snap Out of It! Radio Network, to showcase my program and others. I've interviewed hundreds of luminaries from all walks of life. In 2009, I released an album of songs titled *I Believe.* I wrote the book *Wisdom Wedgies & Life's Little Zingers.* I've written countless articles and been a guest on dozens of radio shows. I also launched my speaking career and produced the "Snap Out of It!" Women's Conference. In 2011, I fulfilled a lifelong dream of singing for my beloved New York Yankees in Yankee Stadium. I regularly sing for such top organizations as the NBA's Oklahoma City Thunder and the MLB's Houston Astros.

Plans are underway for my one-woman show, *If I Stop, Then Who Am I?* an autobiographical musical journey about the illusion of distractions and addictions that asks the question: If we stop and let go of all that we currently believe to be true about who we are and what we are, then who will we be?

Life is indeed full of choices and illusions. What I know today is this: If we do not examine our illusions, they can take us far, far away from our intended path. I also know, however, that it's never too late to make a different choice, never too late to question what we currently believe to be true, and certainly never too late to lean into and accept the unfamiliar and the unknown.

I thank God every day for the works of Eldon Taylor, for he has helped me to reshape, reprogram, and regain my courage and confidence, which ultimately helped me to see who I truly am. You could say he helped me wake up, stand up, and snap out of it!

DeDe Murcer Moffett,
keynote speaker/author/talk-show host/recording artist
www.dedemurcermoffett.com
Wake Up, Stand Up & Snap Out of It!

My Warm, Fuzzy Feelings

Let me share with you some other stories from people seeking improvement in their lives who have worked with InnerTalk. These represent a partial source of some of my own warm, fuzzy feelings, but hopefully you will relate to at least one and gain the confidence necessary to take that step called change. We have run the studies, dozens of them, as I mentioned earlier. Still, there is truth in the words of Nathanael Emmons: "Any fact is better established by two or three good testimonials, than by a thousand arguments."

"I deserve!" They are the two most life-changing and most precious words in the English language. When you say, "I deserve" and really mean it in your heart, your life will change forever, permanently, and for the better! When you feel that "you deserve," you will no longer eat yourself senseless and numb, because you know that "you deserve" to treat yourself with kindness and with compassion. When you feel like "you deserve," you will honor yourself and respect others and no longer be a doormat for the convenience of friends and family. When you state loudly and proudly to the Universe, to God, and to the angels that "you deserve," you open yourself up to unlimited possibilities. I know what I am talking about!

I Do Deserve Better

A few years ago my life was a living hell, but once I summoned the courage and told myself that I do indeed deserve better, my life was on the road to healing and to new discovery! With the help of Eldon Taylor and his InnerTalk programs, I was able to transform my life from the inside out! I was once trapped in an abusive marriage, thinking I deserved to be treated like dirt. I weighed 350 pounds and ate all of my frustration and my rage. I knew deep down that I was smart, funny, and could do anything, but I was verbally beaten down so badly that I forgot who I was.

That all changed the moment it hit me that I really do deserve. No one could take this step for me! I had to reach out for help, and Eldon Taylor had the tools for the inner change that I was praying for! The very first program that I ordered was *Weight Loss Now*. I thought that being fat was my problem, but being obese was just a symptom of my low self-esteem. I listened to the InnerTalk programs religiously, and slowly I began to see a change in how I viewed food. I began losing weight, and I gained more self-esteem, but I still felt like I needed more encouragement. This time I ordered *Releasing Co-Dependent Patterns*. I learned that my husband could not abuse me without my permission, and once I withdrew my permission, my life really started to take off! For the first time in a long while,

I felt worthwhile and worth the work that I was doing to change my behavior.

Become Your Own Hero

I continued listening to the programs, and I added to my InnerTalk library. I ordered *Soaring Self-Esteem, Personal Power, Releasing Anger,* and the most powerful program in my arsenal, *Ending Self-Destructive Patterns.* I slowly was changing and finally had the courage to divorce my husband and to take on my own life. You see, when you decide to take personal responsibility for yourself, and for your actions, you become your own hero! I finally realized that I had the power all along but needed the help from InnerTalk to help me on my journey!

When I listened to these fine audio programs, I found out that I was living under false programming—false programming that I was calling my life! I took the first step and called Dr. Taylor for help.

Now I am happier, healthier, calmer,
thinner (150 pounds lighter),
but most important—I feel whole!

Now, it is up to you to realize that you can take on your own personal power and to take on your life. I know that sometimes you only feel a glimmer of what your life could be like . . . but hold on! Be true to your real self, and reach out to Dr. Taylor and his very kind staff. They are more than willing to help you along your new and very exciting journey of self-discovery. You are a loving, capable, funny, smart, and worthwhile person. You deserve the best that life has to offer! Stop settling for less than what you can give! Life isn't meant to be tolerated and suffered through. Life is to be lived, with excitement and joy! Start taking responsibility for your own health, wealth, and happiness. *Believe me, the journey will be worth it!*

Jackie Howell,
Utah

●◉●

I first learned about the power of the mind when I was a teenager. After learning that I could change my life by changing my thoughts, I began to guard my thoughts more carefully and, most important, I started taking the time to monitor what was going into my mind. Knowing that my subconscious mind has the power to shape my destiny, I started looking for ways to put more positive ideas into my subconscious mind. One day I was fortunate enough to hear about Eldon Taylor's InnerTalk programs. Since then, I have been hearing his CDs regularly in the areas of weight loss, self-esteem, and prosperity.

As a result of hearing these wonderful subliminal recordings, *I have lost and kept off 35 pounds, my self-esteem has risen considerably, and my prosperity knows no limits.* I am constantly blessed by good things happening to me as a result of the prosperous thoughts my mind has been programmed with.

About eight months after my daily practice of hearing Eldon Taylor's *Prosperity and Abundance* InnerTalk program, I was fortunate enough to win $50,000 in my state lottery, which I used to pay for laser eye surgery and to take care of other obligations I had at the time. Since then, I have prospered in business and in my social life. I attribute this good fortune to the continual use of these products, because dedicated use has allowed me to replace my old self-limiting thoughts with healthy, vibrant, and more creative thoughts, which have spilled out into every aspect of my life and continue to bless me each day.

These days I dedicate my free time to speaking and teaching others about the prosperous power of creative thinking, and I regularly give out Eldon Taylor's audio programs at various seminars I give a few times a year. Some of my friends have told me about how these products have changed their lives, and I owe it all to the power of the subconscious mind.

Eddie Coronado,
California

(After the first edition of *Choices and Illusions* was published in 2007, I heard from many people about how this book had changed their lives. However, I also learned that while most people enjoy and want more, some people are put off by the stories of others. For this reason, if you would like to read more, please see Appendix C or visit the website **www.innertalk.com.**)

It's Your Choice

This has largely been the story of my journey of personal growth. It might be said that much of it is self-serving, and that's fair enough, I guess, but equally true is the fact that each of us can genuinely only speak to each other from our own experience.

The stories of all of the people in this book and the appendix are themselves examples of how each of us can empower ourselves if we only but choose to believe in the unlimited power within. The common denominator with every story is a simple truth: believing in yourself does matter!

It is my hope that by sharing just a few of the stories that have been sent to me and by telling my own, that you the reader will gain some insight into the how, what, and why of self-imposed limitations and at least a couple of solid exit strategies for leaving those limitations in the past, if not for yourself, then for someone you care about.

A Word of Caution

It is a common tactic of naysayers, especially those with any so-called academic clout, to dismiss ideas of merit by using a tactic easily described this way: "One good belly laugh is worth a thousand syllogisms." This approach seeks to discredit not only through "the subtraction game" but also through immense ridicule. It may take courage to ignore this tactic if it comes your way, but that too is perfectly within your power. You will never know what you might imagine if you never think the question: *What would I do if I knew I could not fail?* You will never achieve a goal if you cannot imagine it. You will never break out of self-imposed or "chicken" learned limitations if a little criticism or ridicule dissuades you. Again, I repeat because it cannot be overstated, *within you is the power!*

CHAPTER 18

◦◈◦◈◦◈◦

CONCLUSION

"Character cannot be developed in ease and quiet. Only through experience of trial and suffering can the soul be strengthened, vision cleared, ambition inspired, and success achieved."

— HELEN KELLER

There are a few slogans, words from the wise, that I try to remain in touch with. Robert H. Schuller said, "Better to do something imperfectly than to do nothing flawlessly." The words of Jerome: "Begin to be now what you will be hereafter." And finally, Napoleon Hill states: "Both poverty and riches are the offspring of thought."

It is written that each of us is a gift from God, and all that we become is our way of returning that gift. I am reminded of a line from a scene in the inspirational fiction work by Angelina Heart, *The Teaching of Little Crow*. In the scene, the hero of the story has a moment of enlightenment as a result of understanding that "[e]very blessed and loving thing you freely put out to the world, whether it be thought, feeling, words, deeds, or money, returns with more of its kind." He pauses and then thinks, *"No wonder Jesus Christ instructed us to love our enemies. What we send out must come back to the creator, magnified."*

The movie *The Celestine Prophecy* has a beautiful scene that is visually portrayed even better than in the book, in my opinion. In this scene, the ninth insight shows itself as a result of those receiving energy sending it back to the sender. The energy grows exponentially in this exchange. If you think of this energy as the unconditional love energy that begins with creation and animates all, then it is easy to see how sending it back would increase it.

Dr. Joe Rubino, in his book *Restore Your Magnificence,* reminds us that the origins of self-doubt are often the result of misinterpretations of self or limited awareness. In his words:

> *"Misinterpretations damage self-esteem and run your life. Freedom comes from reinterpreting your past with compassion for your humanity and that of others."*

My Journey

This has been a book sharing both a little bit of myself and what I have learned, interpreted, and reinterpreted many times. I was born into a religious family. I worked hard, attended church every Sunday, studied, and reread what I had studied. At a very young age, I was ordained in the priesthood, but many things didn't quite square with logic, reason, or consistency of the doctrine. I continued seminary studies but asked hard questions. I remembered what I was supposed to remember so I could take exams and get *A*'s. However, when it came to term grades, I was admittedly shocked to find I'd flunked. Well, I was not abashed, so I took the matter up with the academic authorities, and during review was informed that the grade would be changed to an *A* provided I never came back. It seems I had become a disturbing force in the classroom.

I took my *A* and left seminary. I became quite bitter and agnostic, if not atheistic. For many years I enjoyed beating up the so-called theological scholars. I lost myself completely. I forgot the miracles in my life and focused on the inadequacies of organized religion, the club that demanded your dues. Then came my awakening, not all at once, but slowly over time. Fortunately, the Universe was patient. I found myself writing philosophical proofs for a Divine Creator and rereading all the sacred literature. In my small book *Exclusively Fabricated Illusions,* I finally set forth the problem that in my view disappoints so many people—the exclusive role of authority, which says, "I have the only right way, and if you fail to follow it, you'll _____!" (You get the picture.)

In the sacred documents of all living religions is a fountain of truth. In the Bible it is said this way: "Whatever you do unto the least of them, you have done unto yourself." Martin Luther King, Jr., once stated, "[W]e must all learn to live together as brothers or we will all perish together as fools." In that interrelated whole exist all of us. We may have been taught differently in our own little chicken yards, but the fact is simple: we are all one.

"Whatever you do unto the least of them,
you have done unto yourself."

Maximizing Your Mind's Awesome Power

I hope this work has shed some light on how and why we might find ourselves limiting our own realizations and beliefs and therefore reality. The mind is an absolutely awesome power, and we still don't know its potential. We do know that it modulates the body in many ways and can be our best friend or our own worst enemy. I would encourage you to take whatever you have gleaned from this book and continue in your progress to becoming all that you might be. I would suggest that you begin with reflection, questioning any and all thoughts that limit your potential good for self and society. I do strongly urge you to follow the good-deed theme presented earlier, together with the other suggestions for improving the quality of your life.

I also urge you to begin meditating. Meditation is a powerful tool; it is, after all, getting quiet and listening to the still, small voice within. "Be still and know." It's easy to meditate and quite natural as well. Begin by choosing some simple word and repeat it with each exhalation. Just close your eyes, relax back, let go, and clear your mind by repeating something like "peace" with every exhalation. Soon the mind stills, and a new vista of feeling and thought manifests. If you find this difficult to do, or if you wish to learn how you can use this state to further your personal growth, I encourage you to pick up my book *Self-Hypnosis and Subliminal*

Technology. In it I explain the connection between hypnosis and meditation, provide simple instructions, and give you a variety of techniques you can practice. But whether or not you decide to explore this, I do urge you to seek that inner noetic sense of your real being, life's true meaning and value—in short, seek the "peace which passeth understanding," for within this space your higher self emerges.

So, in conclusion, we have convoluted the model. Our purpose is service, not taking. Our warm, fuzzy feeling provides peace, balance, harmony, and improved health. Our recognition of the good in all works much like a magnet to attract the right people and things into our lives, including our most enduring and loving relationships. Our prosperity is assured, for in the moment we always have everything we need, and ironically, we keep getting more when we stop trying to just make money. We bring our best with joy to whatever our task may be, and that is not only recognized but rewarded. We are not pitiful creatures here to suffer, but rather gifts from our Creator endowed with true co-creative powers. Our belief propels our lives with optimism and integrity, not a pack full of bad-luck fortune cookies. We give to give, not out of some codependent bargain based on what we get back or control of some kind over another. We forgive and release blame; no more "get even and evener." We take responsibility and improve every day in every way.

Change Those Subconscious Beliefs

One of the material findings from my work and the InnerTalk technology that is worth mentioning is how it works. But first let me explain why this is important. When exit polls are performed following many motivational events, the vast majority of attendees report a positive result and pledge to incorporate their new tools and learnings into their lives upon returning home. However, when following up with these people a month later, we discover that indeed most have not applied what they learned. There are always reasons (excuses) for this failure. Some may say something like, "Well, I thought about it, and it's just not right for my personality." Others claim that they simply have not had the time. Some say they tried, but it just didn't work. For the most part, it's all excuses. The fact is, just as I have suggested, if your inner mind (subconscious) does not believe it, you won't do it. Remember the "million dollar" characterization and Mr. Bill Gates? No amount of flashing lights, brilliant mirrors, loud music, and rah-rah alone can persuade the subconscious to let go of its adaptations and mechanisms. In other words, if you stand in front of the mirror and say to yourself, meaningfully and deliberately, statements that the subconscious disagrees with, it is only a matter of time before the inner talk (self-talk) begins to undermine those statements. Then in some automatic, servo-loop way, the old behaviors just reassert themselves and that's the end, at least for the moment, of the desired change.

With the InnerTalk technology, all we need to do is listen, and we can play it in the background while we watch television or even sleep. One hour a day for 30 days, and somehow something just magically seems to change. The change can seem dramatic and often happens even faster than expected, as you saw in the last chapter in the comments sent to me by users of InnerTalk. The reason for this seeming magic, and it's not magic at all, is that the subliminal beliefs in the subconscious mind have been massaged sufficiently to allow the stream of consciousness or self-talk to reflect the affirmations contained on the InnerTalk program, and voilà, change is easy. And now you can try this for yourself, for included with this book is my InnerTalk program entitled *Unlimited Personal Power.* Simply play this program in the background as you go about your day, and see for yourself the benefits of changing your self-talk. (The affirmations for this program have been included in Appendix D).

For the record, I have often been asked why we have more than 400 titles. Are we attempting to create perfect people? I believe you and everyone else is already perfect, albeit many may be asleep or have not fully awakened to their divine potential. No, the reason we have as many titles as we do is to meet everyone where they are. Indeed, one of the original driving forces behind title development came from prison systems. Inmates wanted bodybuilding, weight lifting, and so forth. Fine, I reasoned, and we'll include the forgiveness set and esteem/responsibility elements in all. We did. In other words, the essential elements to taking responsibility, forgiving, appreciating, and otherwise beginning the process of awakening is on every single program we make, regardless of title. In fact, let me share a personal story with you, as it may shed additional light on my personal perspective.

The Buddha, Edgar Cayce, and Jesus

Some years ago I was asked to speak at a prestigious gathering of hypnotherapists, hypnotists, and psychotherapists. Every year for several years I had spoken at this event, so of course I accepted. The night before I arrived was the typical welcoming banquet for all participants. After the meal an older woman, who was a staff member of the school sponsoring the event and seated at the head table, lit a cigarette. A man in the audience promptly stood, walked to her table, jerked the cigarette from the woman's hand, scolded her loudly while suffocating the cigarette in her ashtray, and returned to his seat wagging his finger at her all the way. She broke into tears and ran from the hall.

To protect this gentle lady's anonymity, I'll just call her Penny. She was a lovely person who went the extra mile helping students at the school, and many in the audience were either students or graduates. She was well known by all, and in my book, she is a wonderful woman with a golden heart who loved helping others.

I was told of this event before speaking, and I changed my entire presentation there and then. I began with "I want you all to imagine that the word is out, the news has traveled around the world, and all know that the best of the best in health-care professionals are gathered here today to share and sharpen their skills. The professionals at this august gathering are noted as the best because their interest is genuinely in helping others. They are sensitive, caring professionals, and they know the power of their words can create wellness as well as dis-ease. They are all aware that the oldest woman on the planet lived well into her hundreds and died only when her doctors told her to stop smoking or die.

"Because this meeting was of such very high caliber, three special people were on their way to attend the gathering. Let's just imagine these three people, say, Buddha, Edgar Cayce, and, if you will, even Jesus. Now, our Buddha is the Buddha of Indian origin, not the Buddha of Chinese history, who is often portrayed as thin. So our Buddha is plump. Cayce, the well-known mystic healer who made literally thousands of readings while in a trance, healing as many people, is a chain smoker. Jesus' well-known statement, paraphrased, says it all: 'It's not what you put in your mouth, but what comes out of it, that will be your undoing.'"

I continued, "So here are our three visitors. They have influenced and healed the lives of more people than anyone can count, and here is what is going to happen. One-third of you will run to Buddha and tell him you can help him lose weight. One-third will run to Cayce and inform him that you can help him stop smoking, and, by the way, you'll tell them both that if they do not do something about it, it will kill them. The remaining third will no doubt offer to assist in keeping Jesus kosher, for everyone knows the story wherein Jesus is caught eating the wrong bread on the Sabbath—and he was, after all, a rabbi."

I went on following this introduction to point out how wrong it was for Penny to have been humiliated and treated in such an undignified manner the night before. I pointed out that judging people, and even possibly suggesting sickness on them, in this way was irresponsible. I received quite nice applause but was never invited back to speak.

Waking Up

The bottom line for me is not about the usual concerns regarding body image and so forth. No, as a matter of fact one is much more likely to experience dis-ease as a result of a psychological predisposition, including how we handle stress and so on, than from enjoying chocolate. For me, it's all about waking up and claiming your true divine potential. Sometimes this happens one small step at a time, as with the longest journey of Lao-tzu. One success, whether it's winning at basketball or losing weight, can lead to building more confidence and empowering individuals to believe in themselves. That's why at InnerTalk the motto is, "When believing in yourself matters." This builds quality of life, and quality of life is, after all, what we all ultimately define as a successful life.

InnerTalk . . . when believing in yourself matters.™

Now, whether or not you ever use an InnerTalk program, I challenge you to take positive steps as soon as you put this book down. It might be easy for you to just sort of wait until tomorrow to begin to practice the simple fundamentals suggested here. Tomorrow never comes. Begin right now to take steps to actively practice forgiving and forgetting. Begin now to seek out opportunities to do at least two good turns every day. Get some paper or buy a diary and begin to write down those little "helps" that you give to others. Write down your feelings. When you go to bed each evening, think about the day and record your good deeds. Take those thoughts to bed with you. I promise that you'll be surprised by what happens to your sleep, dreams, health, and happiness.

Memory Landmarks

You may even discover memory landmarks that bring back warm, fuzzy feelings. I experienced one recently with a big smile on my face, and my wife asked what the smile was for. I told her of a clerk who had gone out of his way to help me, despite my error. You see, the last time I had seen him was months before. On that day he was down. His body language, facial expression, and general demeanor spoke for him. When I stepped up to the counter, I simply said, "Joe, what are you doing? You look younger!"

At first he looked puzzled.

"No, I'm serious, Joe. You look like you've taken ten years off." (Joe is approximately sixty.) "Even your complexion looks younger and healthier. What are you doing?" I continued.

Joe replied, "You really think so, Doc?"

"Yes, Joe. I mean, look at yourself, you're even standing straighter, and that smile on your face must be telling your brain to turn up all those good neurochemicals," I responded as I watched Joe follow the suggestion and stand straighter with a smile.

"Well, Doc, you've made my day," he said. "You need to come back more often," he added with a rich smile and gleam in his eyes.

My lovely wife added, "So this is another of your 'fake it till you make it' strategies, and Joe made it."

Indeed, that's where we all begin. We make the choice to smile, engage the world with joy and awe, do our good turns, and otherwise share the love with which we fill our hearts to overflowing. In the beginning, we may need to fake it. Sooner or later, though, because the brain actually does turn on positive, healthy neurochemicals as a mechanical reaction to smiling, our faking takes hold and we become what we pretend to be.

I know you get the picture, so please begin to act now. Life is a miracle and living a joy! You are a miracle and a gift, and you repay the gift by being all that you were created to be. Soar, my Eagle Friend.

⊙◈⊙◈⊙◈⊙

EPILOGUE

Enlightenment or empowerment, call it what you will, is only possible when you comprehend fully the power of your mind. It is also important, however, to understand and appreciate the lengths that certain groups will go to in order to turn this mind power against you, so that your mind is in their control.

There are those who choose to focus on the positive, believing that they already understand the dangers of marketers, and they have already turned off their televisions. They feel comfortable, believing they have already taken all necessary steps in choosing to just focus on the positive. However, that really is not the smartest approach. Yes, marketers are great mind manipulators, but so are many other groups, such as politicians, reporters, entertainers, and movies. With more and more marketing being embedded in movies themselves, soon advertisements could well become a thing of the past.

And then, on top of all of this is the very fact that we humans are herd animals. Although you may be careful of what goes into your mind, you will have many friends and family members who are not. These people will talk to you, and all that has happened is that the mind programming has just come via another step. The recluse is actually very rare, but it is only by being a total recluse that you can avoid mind manipulation. Not that I am advocating a reclusive lifestyle—far from it. What I am really saying is that it is impossible to avoid the manipulations of others, and so it is only by understanding your own mind and psychology and being constantly vigilant that you can even begin to become your own person. It is only by paying close attention to your own life experiences that you can begin to answer the big questions, such as Who am I? Why am I here? and What is my purpose in life?

I have now presented you with the big picture, which includes the following aspects:

- Showing you how your choices may not be your own;

- Demonstrating how pervasive mind manipulation has become;

- Exposing the fact that there are many areas where "they" have already won the battle for your mind;

- Revealing a much larger picture of the power of your mind;

- Encouraging you to examine your own thoughts to find the dissonance and, therefore, discover your own truth;

- Leading you through some of the miracles in my life in the hope that you will remember the miracles in your own and so assisting you in finding more meaning in your own life; and

- Providing my thoughts on the best tools for reversing negative effects and enhancing your own personal empowerment.

Whatever your thoughts on God, spirituality, and the afterlife, and whether you believe in such things or not, there is no escaping the truth that life is an amazing experience. We owe it to ourselves to maximize this opportunity in any way that we can. As you can see, I believe that the key to maximizing our experience rests in the incredible power of your mind. You can foster this power, nurturing it and allowing it to grow, or you can turn it (all of it or just parts of it) over to others. The choice is yours, and that is *not* an illusion!

◉◉◉◉◉◉◉

APPENDIX A

Science of InnerTalk®

InnerTalk is based on more than 25 years of research and development. It is the only such technology to have been repeatedly researched and demonstrated effective by independent universities and institutions around the world. Although this technology was patented under the name *Whole Brain,* it is now more commonly referred to as InnerTalk. Here is a brief overview of a few of the studies that have demonstrated its effectiveness:

1985–1986: In a double-blind study at the Utah State Prison, which was performed by McCusker, Liston, and Taylor, the InnerTalk technology was deemed effective in altering *self-esteem* among inmates. As a result, the Utah State Prison installed and maintains a voluntary tape library for inmates.

1988–1990: Cosmetic surgeon R. Youngblood and surgical staff tested the effect of the InnerTalk *Pre and Post Operative* program on 360 patients. They reported a decrease in anesthetic requirements of 32 percent by volume as compared to a historical control group.

1990: In a double-blind study carried out at Colorado State University, it was found that using the InnerTalk program *Freedom from Depression* for more than 17 hours led to a significant decrease on the Beck Depression scale. This study not only shows the effectiveness of the InnerTalk program, but also indicated that the effectiveness of the programs was dosage related.

1990: A double-blind study was carried out at Weber State University on the effects of the InnerTalk program *Freedom from Stress*. The psychological test results showed a significant decrease in stress.

1991: A double-blind study conducted by Professor Peter Kruse at Bremen University in Germany, using a specially created Inner-Talk program, strongly demonstrated the influence of the program on decision making. Kruse said, "The Taylor method works!"

1991: Experimental psychologist Dr. Julian Isaacs investigated the effects of the following InnerTalk programs: *No More Procrastination, Time Management, Confidence Power, Freedom from Stress, Positive Relationships, I Am Assertive,* and *High Self-Esteem.* After three studies, it was concluded that the programs produced significant positive results that were verifiable.

1988–1991: The findings from a pilot longitudinal study on the InnerTalk program for cancer showed that 43 percent of the patients who used the program went into remission. For the other patients, who eventually passed away, the average life span beyond the original prognosis was significantly extended.

1991: A study carried out by Professor R. B. Pelka of Munich University in Germany on an InnerTalk program for weight loss showed average weight losses of 13 pounds in subjects who used the program without following any other kind of diet or exercise regimen.

1993: Diana Ashley at the University of Southern California studied the effect of InnerTalk on academic achievement in a double-blind experiment. Her conclusion found a significant increase in learning among students in the experimental group.

1993: Kim Roche at the University of Phoenix studied the effect of InnerTalk with children diagnosed as having attention deficit hyperactive disorder (ADHD) in a double-blind experiment. Her findings indicated a significant positive effect.

1993: Thomas Plante, faculty member of Santa Clara University and former director of mental health services for the Children's Health Council, together with Michael DiGregorio, Gerdenio

Manuel, and Bao-Tran T. Doan of Santa Clara University, evaluated the effect of InnerTalk on test anxiety in a double-blind experiment. The statistical data significantly supported the hypothesis that InnerTalk subliminal technology could be an effective tool in lowering test anxiety.

1997: Under the direction of Maurice P. Shuman, Jr., general director of Special Programs of Instruction, a pilot study was conducted by Duval County Public School system at the Pre-Trial Detention Facility in Jacksonville, Florida. Twenty-two incarcerated juveniles participated in a study program using InnerTalk programs designed to assist in preparation for GED examination. The GED final test results show that 18 of the 22 troubled students passed the full GED examination.

1998: Combining InnerTalk *Weight Loss* audio and video with Echo-Tech audio and a special nutritional program developed and marketed by Oxyfresh International, Dr. Harbans S. Sraon, a biochemical geneticist of the University of California, Irvine, conducted a 90-day weight-loss study. Dr. Sraon coached each subject to visualize their clear goal in terms of body fitness and reviewed progress weekly. Sraon reported that 90 percent of the subjects (10 men and 15 women) lost significant amounts of weight.

1998: Under the direction of Dr. Jose Salvador Hernandez Gonzalez and on behalf of the Institute of Mexican Social Services (Medicas), 25 patients were exposed to both video and audio *Freedom from Dental Anxiety* tapes for 30 minutes prior to treatment and 30 minutes during treatment. The conclusion was as follows: "The use of InnerTalk before an integral odontologic treatment is 100 percent effective, reducing patient's anxiety and the noise made by the high speed hand piece used in this type of work, and furthermore, reducing the pain suffered by comparison to previous experience." The report goes on to recommend InnerTalk: "Therefore it is convenient to promote, among dental surgeons, the use of InnerTalk to improve their patients' comfort and achieve a better collaboration to treatments."

2002 (September): Jane Alexander, independent journalist and researcher in the United Kingdom, ran her own study on the efficacy of InnerTalk. Independent testers worked with *Ultra Success Power, Neat and Tidy, Attracting the Right Love Relationship,* and *Jealousy.* All of the testers reported positive results.

2002 (November): Jane Alexander investigated several alternative methods for weight loss. Not only did she find significant weight loss using the CD for weight loss, she also did a price comparison between the different alternative treatments. Her cost comparison on a per pound of weight loss basis showed costs of £26/lb for acupuncture (approx. $41.60), £11.42/lb for hypnotherapy (approx. $18.27), £29.28/lb for homeopathy (approx. $46.85), and £3.28/lb for InnerTalk (approx. $5.25).

2003: The results of a UK trial on the InnerTalk program titled *Breast Enlargement* was published in *What Medicine,* summer 2003 issue. "This trial involved 15 women and resulted in approximately 2cm of breast growth and a fuller cup size within 30 days. Women also reported a 'tingling sensation,' similar to that experienced in puberty."

Numerous clinical studies with single and multiple subjects have also found effectiveness with InnerTalk in areas as diverse as anorexia and dyslexia. Additionally, InnerTalk has been credited by professional coaches for significantly contributing to winning sports events ranging from football championships to national and Olympic judo medals.

◉◉◈◉◈◉◉

APPENDIX B

Utah Prison Study: Abstract of Findings

by Charles F. McCusker, Ph.D.

Thirty-eight male residents (average age 23) from the unit at the Utah State Prison completed the Thurstone Temperament Schedule in a voluntary participatory study. Following administration, subjects were randomly placed in one of three groups (experimental, 14; placebo, 13; and control, 11). The experimental group received and played a subliminal tape for 20 days. The placebo group received and played a similar sounding tape without an embedded subliminal message, while the control group had no tape exposure. At the end of 20 days a second Thurstone Temperament Schedule was administered. In the experimental group, 5 subjects remained who had completed the procedure, 3 in the placebo group, and 8 in the control group. Others were lost due to discharges or unwillingness to participate.

In a comparison of the experimental and control groups, the following results were obtained. The dominance scale scores decreased while the reflective and stability scale scores increased in the experimental group (desired effects). The dominance scale scores increased while the reflective scale scores decreased in the control group. These are interesting results across groups. In the experimental group, these results would be predicted by focus of the embedded subliminal messages. In the placebo group, the opposite effect obtained may be explained by the fact that they (the subjects) listened to a tape without a message and felt no change. They obtained no reinforcement to continue and possibly experienced some frustration.

It is emphasized that this pilot study had limitations, especially in terms of implementation and sample size.

It is not the intention of the experimenters to generalize beyond the obtained results. It must be emphasized, however, that to evaluate an incarcerated population was a unique opportunity; to our knowledge this was the first time subliminal technology has been evaluated with this population. The results indicated change and strongly suggest the need for further research with benefit to these individuals and society in general, as this technology is better understood and applied in a wide variety of applications and settings.

Experimental			Control		
Predifferences to postdifferences			Predifferences to postdifferences		
Scale Movement	Variable	Rate of Change	Scale Movement	Variable	Rate of Change
↑	Stability	+3.4	↑	Stability	+8
↑	Reflectivity	+2.6	↓	Reflectivity	-1.0
↓	Dominance	-2.7	↑	Dominance	+1.4

Figure 26

◦◉◦◉◦◉◦

APPENDIX C

Personal-Empowerment Stories

I'm writing to let you know how absolutely thrilled I am with the results achieved with the InnerTalk products. My journey began with *Self-Esteem, Success, Prosperity,* and *Self-Confidence.* My results came rapidly, as I don't do things by halves and initially used the CDs for extended periods of time on a recurring basis. The results have been amazing. These products have definitely changed the quality of my life. I feel so much more joy, happiness, and gratitude—my confidence is sky high—my outlook is totally optimistic, and I am razor sharp and focused and constantly visualize only the best. The actions required to achieve my goals are now performed almost automatically, and as a result my business has improved dramatically. I honestly feel I have come to a place now where I am unstoppable and anything is possible. My advice to anyone looking to achieve improvement in any area of their lives is to try the products for themselves. I warmly congratulate Eldon Taylor on his accomplishments and contribution in the area of self-development and personal growth. *These products work!*

Daniel Calleja,
Australia

The first time I invested in the InnerTalk CDs, I was a bit skeptical. I just went ahead and told myself to give it a try. After continually playing the CDs, I can see and feel the changes that are happening around me.

I found myself being more confident, having the ability to make decisions more constructively, and more positive vibes circulate around my environment.

The effect is more apparent in my daughter. She has matured faster and shows signs of vast developmental skills compared to her peers.

Overall, after five months of listening to the CDs, I must say there is indeed a positive improvement in our lives. Thank you.

Ranjit Singh,
Malaysia

◦◉◦

Before I started working with the InnerTalk programs, I felt like a rapidly aging 51-year-old spinster—gaining weight and going through the menopause. I just assumed life would be downhill all the way from then on.

I came across the InnerTalk programs quite by accident and decided to use them on myself as an experiment before I would think about using the programs in my complementary medicine practice. At that time, I was keen to change where my life was going, both physically and mentally.

The first CD I used was *Using Metabolism to Melt Fat.* I had not "dieted" as such for 25 years, as I know that dieting makes you fat by lowering the metabolic rate. Also, in the past, I never lost weight where I needed to—from my middle and legs—but only from my bust. However, my weight had crept up over the years from 8 stone 4 lbs (116 pounds) in my 20s and 30s to a whopping 10 stone (140 pounds). I thought realistically, I might get down to 9 stone 3 pounds (129 pounds—the maximum recommended weight for my height of 5'0").

How wrong I was! Amazingly, after listening to the CD for 6 weeks, I lost 7 pounds with no change in eating pattern. Even more amazingly, it came off my waist and legs. I then stopped listening to the CD and have never used it since. I realized, however, that I was still losing weight, around 3 or 4 pounds over 6 months. One year after first listening to the CD, I weighed in at 9 stone 2 pounds (128 pounds). I then lost another 10 pounds rather too quickly while moving.

For the first time in my adult life, I have a normal hip-waist ratio and am no longer "blob-shaped." I have maintained my weight at 8 stone 4 pounds to 8 stone 7 pounds (116 pounds to 119 pounds) for more than two years now. The only problem is eating enough to prevent further weight loss. (I do not want to be too skinny.) Hardly any weight came off my bust, my hips are down from 34" to 33", I've lost 5" or 6" from my waist, and my legs are quite a "normal" size.

I believe the CD has permanently "rejigged" my metabolism at a time in my life when I thought the middle-age spread was inevitable. Though I am back to the weight I was when I was younger, it is distributed in a much better shape. My friends are all amazed.

Since then I have used a number of different InnerTalk programs. I had suffered from headaches for years, so decided to use the *Freedom from Headaches.* As soon as I started to use the CD, I felt a pleasant tingling in my head and a calm feeling. Every time I use the CD, I notice when I look in the mirror how relaxed and soft my face looks—better than a facial. The headaches disappeared and have not returned. Nowadays I do get the odd headache, but nowhere near as severe, and the CD soon sees them off.

For years I had wanted to move, but it seemed impossible. I was afraid of being stuck in a chain, or being "gazumped" [someone making a higher offer] after incurring legal expenses, etc. My little daydream was that I would go view a house. The vendor, a lady on her own, would take a shine to me, announce that she wanted me to buy her house and no one else. She would then take it off the market so no one could gazump me. Meanwhile a cash buyer, a man, would knock on my door and offer to buy my house. There would be no "chains" involved . . . if only!

That was the dream, but it would need a miracle in a cut-throat, overheated housing market. I started to listen to *Expect a Miracle.* Two months later, I saw a suitable house and . . . it was exactly as in the dream! It all actually happened—the lady vendor, the cash buyer—as in the dream.

There was inevitably some stress attached to the move; my hair really suffered. I had always been known for my long, thick, curly hair. As the menopause approached, it became thin, dry with a few gray hairs, and the curl seemed to have gone. With the house move, it started thinning at an alarming rate; the hairdresser said there was nothing I could do about it and cut quite a lot off. How wrong he was. After the first few plays of *Freedom from Hair Loss,* there was a strong, pulling sensation on my scalp. After a few days when I washed my hair, the curls sprang back. I can honestly say my hair has never thickened up so quickly or grown so fast as over the next few weeks. One or two friends asked if I had started to color my hair because even the few gray hairs seemed to vanish. When I next went to the hairdresser, he was amazed at the difference in the quality and strength of the hair and could not believe that a CD could do this.

Last year I fell downstairs and damaged my shoulder very badly. The pain was severe and constant, night and day, for the first few months. I spent all my days for the first few months lying down. Even the Magnessage (bio-magnet) scarcely touched it. I found if I could get into one position and listen to *Natural Pain Relief,* by the time the CD finished I would be very comfortable and get some sleep. Without the CD I would have needed painkillers—something I prefer to avoid.

Although I do not suffer from inhalation allergies, some of my clients have an allergy to my cats. I therefore played *Freedom from Allergies* when treating those clients. I found that while I was playing this CD, my breathing became deeper and more relaxed, and my clients noticed an improvement in their allergy response.

Two friends used the *Natural Breast Enlargement* CD, both in their 50s. One "gained an inch" in 6 weeks. The other "went up a cup size." Both say their breasts are firmer and younger looking.

Although I am qualified in various therapies and pretty good on basic medical sciences, I always just bluffed my way through chemistry modules. Thanks to a good memory I could regurgitate the textbook on command, but I never really "got it." When I put the *Concentration* CD on while I was studying, it was as if a combination lock suddenly opened in my brain, and the basic concepts of chemistry were blindingly simple. I finally "got it" and can now handle the subject with ease.

I had always believed that being rich was not a good thing and felt slightly uncomfortable in wanting to have money when there were so many people in the world less fortunate than myself. However, after using the *Prosperity and Abundance* program, I found myself thinking about this in a different way. Now I believe that if, or rather when, I become rich, I will have the resources to help people.

I had an interesting experience when playing *Opening and Balancing the Chakras* during a massage session—the client suddenly said she could see colors. Although I never use the CDs without explaining what they are and obtaining consent, I had not actually told her what specific one had just started to play. The next time I saw her, she immediately recognized the CD as the same one because once again she could see these colors.

Releasing Anger always makes me feel very calm and relaxed when I listen to it.

All in all, using the InnerTalk CDs has helped me to move with relative ease; my friends all say that I am more confident; the excess 20 pounds has stayed off, giving me a better figure than when I was younger; and my hair has gone back to its thicker, curlier, premenopausal state. I am now 54 years old and feel much younger. I used to be pessimistic, but now I am optimistic.

Best of all, I still have several more InnerTalk CDs waiting to be explored—they are my most valued possessions.

Thank you!

Elizabeth Christie,
United Kingdom

⚫

I have been using InnerTalk products for more than a year now, and I am still benefiting from them. I would not have done so well in juggling my life without the help of InnerTalk. A few of my regular topics are *Concentration, Powerful Memory, Accelerated Learning and Study, Power Learning and Memory, Time Management,* and *Relaxation*. I feel that I have so much enthusiasm to learn at school, and I am surprised to find myself having so much energy to keep up with my busy schedule. Life in New York is hectic, especially now that I'm in the nursing program for becoming a registered nurse. Health professions in the U.S. are not easy. It was very competitive just to get in, and now I have to worry about staying in the program. We have lots of homework, exams with high passing grades, and long clinical rotation hours. However, I feel relaxed and calm, and I always know what to do to keep myself on schedule and also at the same time to stay healthy. I realize that I am not as panicked and fearful as I used to be.

In the past, the block that I had was self-limitation. Lack of self-esteem, fears, and worries were the major things that limited my success. Now, I have confidence in myself. I also have noticed my improvement in writing papers after listening to *Creative Writing*. I was never fond of written assignments; they are my worst nightmares. Though I am still not very much interested in them, I can handle them much better now. I worry less, and I now hand in my papers on time. I can even concentrate better in generating my ideas. So far, I have done very well on all of them. Thank you, InnerTalk, for helping me to help myself. And I thank myself for having taken the initiative to try out the products.

Joon Theen Ng,
New York

❄◈❄

Jeron has a strong desire to represent his school for basketball competition. However, because of his physique and height, chances look rather slim. Knowing how the other InnerTalk *Learning* CDs have helped him in his learning attitude and performance, Jeron started listening to the *Basketball* CD to perfect his skills. Barely two weeks later, his perfect shooting skills, baseline to baseline, etc., has earned him a place on the school team, and he is of course playing competitive basketball right now. Thanks to InnerTalk *Basketball* and *Winning Sports Performance*.

Jodee, Jeron's sister, has also used *Winning Sports Performance* to garner her strong win in the Junior Girls' Open (under 10) Table-Tennis Tournament organized by the Singapore Sports Council. She emerged as Top 8 in the national competition, though she was relatively new to this game and it was her first competitive experience. Her strong mental attitude, sporting and winning spirit, perfect performance, instinctive and natural playing, concentration, strong enthusiasm—empowered and enhanced via InnerTalk *Winning Sports Performance* CD—have certainly enabled her first competitive winning track record. Jodee is looking forward to the release of *Table-Tennis* CD from Eldon Taylor to enhance the specific table-tennis skills/strokes for her future endeavors in her competitive journey.

Mr. and Mrs. Bonny Kua,
Singapore

•◉•

I just finished Eldon Taylor's new book, *Choices and Illusions,* which makes a strong case for subliminal learning documented by numerous case studies. I was so taken by this offering and the possibilities it offers concerning reprogramming our minds and bodies by listening to InnerTalk subliminal recordings that I immediately ordered and read one of his earlier books, *Subliminal Learning,* and several InnerTalk CDs. The second book gave me more information about the technology, and the CDs I am listening to regularly.

Either I am highly suggestible or these things actually work. Since listening to *Neat and Tidy,* which I am not, I find myself cleaning and picking up. When I listen to *Powerful Memory,* old memories from long past crop up as if my mind was defragging itself like a computer, and I have a compulsion to do a better job of remembering names, something that was not my forte. I haven't had the CDs for very long. I am going to keep playing them.

Winston Cook,
Idaho,
Co-author, *Incidents Beyond Coincidence*

•◉•

I had a tournament going on so I began listening to the Inner-Talk *Basketball* CD. At that point, the team and I had no training sessions prior to the tournament, so the whole group has been kind of rusty. I noticed that I was improving in every match and doing more things that I usually would not have done. My performance seemed as if I had been training every day; even my coach was surprised. I was also surprised and happy that I haven't made any mistakes during my games. My confidence was very high, and I was very focused during the games. I'm very impressed at the short span of time and speed of change/results achieved by simply diligently listening to the InnerTalk CD.

Adrian Teng,
Singapore
(former member of the national team)

◦◉◦

Three and a half years ago I first started using Eldon Taylor's InnerTalk programs. I was working as a booking agent for music acts, and most of the time I just did not feel very capable. I felt like something was wrong, but I did not know what it was. I felt afraid to move ahead and was aware of the negativity inside but did not know how to deal with it. I had been through the 12-step program for success, had tried using positive affirmations on myself, but nothing had worked. I still felt incomplete, as though there was much more that I could achieve in my life if only I could break through some elusive barrier.

When I first heard about subliminal programs, I was optimistic. I thought I had finally found the technology that could unlock the successful version of myself that was trapped inside. Unfortunately, I did not feel any change with the first subliminal programs I tried. However, I still felt that positive subliminal affirmations could hold the answer. Maybe the first company I had tried had an inferior product and there was more to creating an effective subliminal program than just burying the affirmations under the music.

Then I received a flyer from a local company that spoke highly of a particular brand of subliminal programs, InnerTalk. I phoned the company to get more details and managed to get the phone number for Progressive Awareness, the publishers of InnerTalk.

When I called Progressive Awareness, the customer service representative explained to me the importance of choosing the right program for my particular goal. In discussing my story with her, I decided that what I needed was extra enthusiasm in order to carry through. I was also told that if I played the programs continuously, then I should be aware of some changes taking place within a few days.

I decided to work with *Ultra Success,* and within a few days I noticed that my self-talk had changed from "I can't" to "I can." I found I could picture myself being successful in a big business. I began to feel as though I could overcome any obstacle and find the answer to any problem. I now knew that success in my business meant working smarter, not harder, and I felt up to the challenge. My successes continued, and everyone could see the change in me. Obstacles that I was once afraid of I now had the confidence to handle. My fears were gone, I was making decisions, and I was solving problems, both at work and with my friends. I no longer felt intimidated and found it easy to sell myself and my services.

I was so happy with the changes I had experienced that I shared this technology with friends and family. My sister thought that subliminals were nonsense, but she had had a sleep problem for three years and so agreed to try the InnerTalk *Sleep Soundly* program. Within a short period, she was sleeping well again. I have a friend in sales, and I got him the InnerTalk program, *Powerful Selling and Closing.* My friend is now so happy because he is getting more cash deals than he has ever had. Things have improved so much for him that not only can he now retain sales recruits, but they even come to him without his having to look for them.

I have now ordered a large number of programs and can always tell when I have "hit the nail on the head," because the results happen really fast. I still buy from Progressive Awareness on a regular basis, because I am still exploring "how high is up," to use a term the sales representative introduced me to.

Name withheld,
New Mexico

•◉•

I have been using the CDs since I attended Eldon Taylor's lecture in December 2005. I am a therapist working with autistic and other special-needs persons, and I recommend that my clients use selected CDs based on their child's needs.

Since I have been listening to them myself, I realize that I am more accepting of others in my family, I feel less stressed, and I am able to cope well even in the midst of my hectic schedule. My business has also increased since I am open to the universe around me daily. I am beginning to go back to my early years in that I am able to find the time to appreciate my surroundings and the people in them.

In regards to my clients, I notice through my careful selecting of CDs for them based on their individual needs, my students are maturing in their own way, mentally and physically. They are more focused in their work, and attention spans have increased. Some of the parents have bought CDs for themselves and their other children.

The best thing about these CDs is that they are extremely relaxing. My stress level has been reduced tremendously and also the stress on the parents who have special needs children. They are feeling happy to be with their special needs child, and this helps the behavior modification work to proceed without much stress.

At the moment I am personally using eight CDs, and this is an investment for my life. The quality of my life has improved, especially with my husband. I am able to accept my challenges when I am challenged by my husband within our family life. In August we went to New Zealand for skiing. I attended ski classes at the resort, and I realized that I could not have been prepared for the mental and physical agility needed to endure the ski instructions. If I had done it before 2005, I would have collapsed with a lot of mental and physical stress and definitely lots of arguments with my husband in regards to skiing. Consistently using the CDs daily, even when I was in New Zealand, kept me very focused and concentrated during my ski classes. I choose my CDs every two months based on my needs as a therapist. We can participate in any program or training for our personal needs, but the key to it is to be *consistent* with the choice of training that we have undertaken for our life. So for me personally I would continue to reach out to others to use the CDs for friends and relatives and also for persons with special needs.

Thank you, Eldon Taylor.

> **Mary Anne Joseph Bekking,**
> Malaysia,
> B. Phil. in Education (specializing in autism)
> Therapist for Special Needs Persons
> **www.myautisticmalaysia.com**

●◉●

I just wanted to give you some feedback relative to your "Quantum Younging" work. I know we volunteered to be part of the program, but I just haven't had a chance to have photographs done, and then I completely forgot about it. I am really sorry. On a positive note, I have a few customers who have subscribed directly to your newsletter, and in February and March I got together with them, and the main issue of discussion was the physical changes I have experienced using the InnerTalk programs. I was even bold enough to bring out the wedding photographs and show them. We made some notes, and even I was amazed at the physical changes I have experienced, and thought I would share my discoveries with you.

I have been using the *Ultra Success Power* and *Ending Self-Destructive Patterns* CDs extensively in the last 18 months and the results for me have been wonderful:

- I have had gray hair since I was 27—I am now 34, and I haven't had any gray hair for 12 months.

- My weight has always been erratic, bouncing between 48 and 58 kg (105.6 and 127.6 pounds) which makes me about 5 to 10 kg underweight. I have maintained my weight at 62 kg for 12 months.

- I had an accident which left scarring down the right side of my face when I was 17, and the scar color has noticeably faded for the last 12 months, so much so that the marks are barely noticeable.

- I have no wrinkles left on my face at all.

- This is the most measurable improvement: my bra size has increased by two sizes.

- I used to suffer from migraines and was taking about 8 painkillers a day. I haven't had a migraine for more than 12 months. That might not be a physical change, but the migraines were a result of eye strain due to the intensity of the graphic work I did. I can focus for much longer periods of time now.

I am definitely healthier, stronger, and much more relaxed. Just wanted to let you have some feedback on my physical improvements and experiences with the products.

Mands,
S. Africa

Amanda has all along been very independent with her schoolwork as long as a timetable was given to her. However, lately she has slackened a little. Before things got worse, I decided to give a try to the *Accelerated Learning and Study* CD that my colleague told me about.

After ten days of Amanda's listening, I certainly observed changes in her behavior. She is less obstinate. During the teaching session with her, she is less argumentative and is more willing to accept comments or constructive feedback that I give her. Another great change with her is that Amanda always lacked the initiative to practice her piano, but now she will tell me "Mum, I have not practiced my piano," and the next thing she will do is practice her piano after finishing her homework!

As for Andy, he is more confident and cries less. Last Tuesday, I was taking my rest at home. I observed Andy automatically do his homework. After that he switched on the computer and accessed MSN, which he has *never* done before! Shortly afterward, he went to play the piano! I thought I saw Amanda and not him. My hubby was shocked too. Andy actually remembered and followed what Amanda has been doing. He was learning to log onto the computer for MSN and playing the piano on his own.

Isn't this great! Confidence, powerful memory, self-motivation to learn, do one thing at a time, etc. The InnerTalk CDs work; they deliver what they promise! We love our two kids very much. We are certain that they are now on the right track about learning and will be enjoying each and every day of their learning journey.

Felicianna Tay,
Singapore

◦◉◦

I purchased *Positive Mental Attitude* about one year after I went through a relationship breakup. I could not get myself together. I knew full well that my negative attitude would eventually slay me—but I couldn't stop. A friend found your website and urged me to give it a try. That was almost 6 years ago. Within a few weeks of listening, I felt like it wasn't hard to breathe or smile. I started to feel like me again—until I looked in the mirror. After a year of sobbing, I had let myself go. My skin was nasty, my hair was a mess, and I smoked too much. So I purchased *Forever Young, Fit and Healthy* and listened to it faithfully. Two months later my uncle visited from Florida. He took one look at me and said, "I have my beautiful niece back. Thank God you look healthy again."

Then it came time to ditch the cigarettes. I was smoking at least 30 a day (maybe more). I got the program, and the funniest thing was, I brushed my teeth more, always trying to get the nasty taste out of my mouth. After 8 days I was down to 11 cigarettes, and then I spooked. I really did not want to let them go, so I stopped listening. I stayed with my 11 a day for years after, but I never enjoyed them. They had become a burden. So I dug out the program again, and within 6 weeks it was over.

I have since recommended your programs to some people and purchased some myself for those who I really believed would benefit from them but might not really go all the way to purchase them. One friend became a better bowler. A family member became pregnant after years of fertility issues.

One more thing—*Power Imaging*—hopefully we can get more of them in the future? I purchased the *Optimal Weight Loss* and lost 10 pounds. When I put it on, it was so soothing I did not want it to end. Thank you, Eldon Taylor, for your brilliance. And thank you, Ravinder, for your patience and kindness.

Name withheld,
New York

◦◉◦◉◦◉◦

APPENDIX D

Affirmations for Unlimited Personal Power

I accept myself.

I accept my creation as a miracle.

I am a miracle.

I am created perfectly.

I accept the perfection.

I accept the gift.

I accept the power.

I am powerful.

I am a leader.

I am an example.

I can do anything.

I know I am gifted and creative.

I expect good.

I expect greatness.

I allow creativity.

I accept inspiration.

Success is mine.

I sense opportunities.

I seize opportunities.

I trust myself.

I am good to myself.

I deserve good.

I am good.

I am confident.

I am grateful.

I am respectful.

I am respected.

I acknowledge good in all.

I find the good in all that comes to me.

I am optimistic.

Happiness and success are mine now.

I make it happen.

I am responsible for me.

I take charge.

I tap into my higher power.

I am in touch with myself.

Within me is the answer.

I get out of my own way.

I listen to the small voice within.

Infinite mind is available to me.

I turn things over.

I have lucid dreams.

Dreams provide answers.

I take advantage of
my advantages.

My senses are keen.

My mind is alert.

I imagine success in detail.

I feel it.

I see it.

I hear it.

I can taste it.

I can smell its sweetness.

❀❁❀❁❀❁❀

RECOMMENDED RESOURCES

Arntz, W. (director) 2005. *What the Bleep Do We Know!?* Twentieth Century Fox Home Entertainment.

Bach, R. 1976. *Jonathan Livingston Seagull: A Story.* New York: Avon Books.

Beattie, M. 1986. *Codependent No More: How to Stop Controlling Others and Start Caring for Yourself.* Center City, MN: Hazelden.

Boone, J. A. 1939. *Letters to Strongheart.* Upper Saddle River, NJ: Prentice Hall.

Capra, F. 1996. *The Web of Life: A New Scientific Understanding of Living Systems.* New York: First Anchor.

Cousins, N. 1981. *Anatomy of an Illness: As Perceived by the Patient.* New York: Bantam.

Dyer, W. 2006. *Inspiration.* Carlsbad, CA: Hay House.

——. 2004. *The Power of Intention.* Carlsbad, CA: Hay House.

Foundation for Inner Peace. 1996. *A Course in Miracles.* New York: Viking.

Gill, M. 2000. *Uncommon Sense.* Singapore: Pandora Publishing.

Goswami, A. 2001. *Physics of the Soul: The Quantum Book of Living, Dying, Reincarnation, and Immortality.* Charlottesville, VA: Hampton Roads.

Guillory, W. 1987. *It's All an Illusion.* Salt Lake City, UT: Innovations International.

——. 1985. *Realizations.* Salt Lake City, UT: Innovations International.

Harper, C. L., Jr., ed. 2005. *Spiritual Information: 100 Perspectives on Science and Religion.* West Conshohocken, PA: Templeton Foundation Press.

Hawking, S. W. 1988. *A Brief History of Time.* New York: Bantam.

——. 2001. *The Universe in a Nutshell.* New York: Bantam.

Heart, A. 2005. *The Teaching of Little Crow.* Virgin, UT: Heart Flame Publishing.

Houston, J. 1997. *The Possible Human: A Course in Enhancing Your Physical, Mental and Creative Abilities.* New York: Tarcher/Putnam.

James, William. 2010. *The Compounding of Consciousness.* Whitefish, MT: Kessinger Publishing.

——. 1992. *The Correspondence of William James, Vol. 1–3.* Charlottesville, VA: University Press of Virginia.

——. 1978. *Essays in Philosophy.* Cambridge, MA: Harvard University Press.

Jampolsky, G. 1979. *Love Is Letting Go of Fear.* Berkeley, CA: Celestial Arts.

——. 1983. *Teach Only Love.* New York: Bantam.

Key, W. B. 1977. *Media Sexploitation.* New York: Signet.

Keyes, K., Jr. 1984. *The Hundredth Monkey.* Camarillo, CA: DeVorss.

——. 1980. *The Clam-Plate Orgy.* New York: Signet.

King, G. R. 1934–2003. *The "I Am" Discourses.* Schaumburg, IL: Saint Germain Press.

Krishnamurti, J. 2004. *Beginnings of Learning.* New York: London: Phoenix.

——. 1987. *The Awakening of Intelligence.* New York: Harper & Row.

——. 1991. *The Collected Works of J. Krishnamurti, 1948–1949: Choiceless Awareness.* Dubuque, IA: Kendall/Hunt Publishing Company.

——. 1987. *Krishnamurti to Himself: His Last Journal.* New York: HarperCollins.

——. 1972. *You Are the World.* New York: Harper.

——. 1963. *Life Ahead.* New York: Harper & Row.

Laing, R. D. 1965. *The Divided Self.* New York: Pelican Books.

——. 1976. *The Facts of Life.* New York: Pantheon Books.

——. 1976. *The Politics of Experience.* New York: Ballantine Books.

Langer, E. J. 1990. *Mindfulness.* Cambridge, MA: Perseus Books.

Lewis, C. S. 1961. *The Screwtape Letters.* New York: Macmillan.

Lipton, B. 2008. *Biology of Belief: Unleashing the Power of Consciousness, Matter & Miracles.* Carlsbad, CA: Hay House.

Marie, T. 2005. *Be the Hero of Your Own Game: A Guide to Master the Game of Life.* Ontario, Canada: Tiki Books.

Maslow, A. H. 1971. *The Farther Reaches of Human Nature.* New York: Penguin.

McTaggart, L. 2001. *The Field: The Quest for the Secret Force of the Universe.* New York: HarperCollins.

——. 2001. *The Intention Experiment.* London: Harper Element.

Mill, J. S. 1975. *On Liberty.* New York: Penguin Books.

Oates, D. J. 1991. *Reverse Speech: Hidden Messages in Human Communication.* Indianapolis, IN: Knowledge Systems, Inc.

Packard, V. 1964. *The Hidden Persuaders.* New York: Pocket Books.

Rossi, E. 1993. *The Psychobiology of Mind-Body Healing: New Concepts of Therapeutic Hypnosis.* New York: W. W. Norton & Company.

Rubino, J. 2003. *Restore Your Magnificence: A Life-Changing Guide to Reclaiming Your Self-Esteem.* Boxford, MA: Vision Works Publishing.

Schwartz, G. 2002. *The Afterlife Experiments: Breakthrough Scientific Evidence of Life After Death.* New York: Pocket Books.

Singer, P. 2000. *Writings on an Ethical Life.* New York: HarperCollins.

Springer, S. P., and Deutsch, G. 1997. *Left Brain, Right Brain.* New York: W. H. Freeman and Company.

Talbot, M. 1991. *The Holographic Universe.* New York: HarperPerennial.

Taylor, E. 1992. *Wellness: Just a State of Mind?* Medical Lake, WA: R. K. Books.

——. 1987. *Little Black Book.* Medical Lake, WA: R. K. Books.

Twain, M. 2004. *Letters from the Earth: Uncensored Writings.* New York: HarperCollins Perennial Modern.

Watts, A. 1975. *Psychotherapy East & West.* New York: Vintage.

——. 1966. *The Book: On the Taboo Against Knowing Who You Are.* New York: Pantheon Books.

Wittgenstein, L. 1973. *Philosophical Investigations: Remarks on the Philosophy of Science.* Englewood Cliffs, NJ: Prentice Hall.

Yogananda, P. 1979. *Autobiography of a Yogi.* Los Angeles, CA: Self-Realization Fellowship.

ENDNOTES

Chapter One

1. Kirshnamurti, J. 1991. *The Collected Works of J. Krishnamurti, 1948–1949: Choiceless Awareness.* Dubuque, IA: Kendall/Hunt Publishing Company.

2. Libet, B., Alberts, W. W., and Wright, E. W. 1976. "Responses of Human Somatosensory Cortex to Stimuli Below Threshold for Conscious Sensation." *Science,* 158 (3808), 1597–1600.

3. Du Sautoy, M. 2009. "Neuroscience and Free Will." **http://www.youtube.com/watch?v=N6S9OidmNZM&feature=share**

4. Joseph, R., ed. 2002. *NeuroTheology: Brain, Science, Spirituality, Religious Experience.* San Jose, CA: University Press.

5. Bach, R. 1976. *Jonathan Livingston Seagull: A Story.* New York: Avon Books.

Chapter Two

1. Niemi, M. B. 2009. "Placebo Effect: A Cure in the Mind." *Scientific American.*

2. Hodges, A. G. 2012. *The Obama Confession.* Birmingham, AL: Village House Publishers.

3. Gladwell, M. 2007. *Blink: The Power of Thinking Without Thinking.* New York: Back Bay Books.

4. Hodges, A. G. 2012. *The Obama Confession.* Birmingham, AL: Village House Publishers.

Chapter 3

1. Rein, G., and McCraty, R. 1993. "Local And Non-Local Effects Of Coherent Heart Frequencies on Conformational Changes Of DNA." *Proceedings of the Joint USPA/ IAPR Psychotronics Conference,* Milwaukee, WI.

2. Niemi, M. B. 2009. "Placebo Effect: A Cure in the Mind." *Scientific American.*

3. Ibid.

4. Taylor, E. 2012. *I Believe: When What You Believe Matters.* Carlsbad, CA: Hay House.

5. Lowitt, B. 1999. "Bannister Stuns World with 4-Minute Mile." *St. Petersburg Times Online:* **http://www.sptimes.com/News/121799/Sports/Bannister_stuns_world .shtml.**

Chapter 4

1. Phillips, D. 1994. "Does Belief Influence the Outcome of Certain Diseases?" *The Lancet,* 342: 1142–45.

2. Langer, E. J. 1990. *Mindfulness.* Cambridge, MA: Perseus Books.

3. Locke, S., and Colligan, D. 1986. *The Healer Within: The New Medicine of Mind and Body.* New York: E. P. Dutton.

4. Andersen, S. M., and Chen, S. 2002. "The Relational Self: An Interpersonal Social-Cognitive Theory." *Psychological Review,* 109, no. 4, 619–45.

Chapter 5

1. Kierkegaard, S. 2002. Edited by H. Hong and E. Hong. *The Essential Kierkegaard.* Princeton, NJ: Princeton University Press.

2. Bly, R. 1988. *A Little Book on the Human Shadow.* New York: HarperOne.

3. Korzybski, A. 1994. *Science and Sanity: An Introduction to Non-Aristotelian Systems and General Semantics.* 5th ed. New York: Institute of General Semantics.

Chapter 7

1. Nauert, R. 2007. "The Influence of Subliminal Messages." *Psych Central.* **http://psychcentral.com/news/2007/12/27/the-influence-of-subliminalmessages/1712.html.**

2. Wilson, T. D. 2002. *Strangers to Ourselves: Discovering the Adaptive Unconscious.* Cambridge, MA: Harvard University Press.

3. Carey, B. 2012. "Academic 'Dream Team' Helped Obama's Effort." *The New York Times.* **http://www.nytimes.com/2012/11/13/health/dream-team-of-behavioral-scientists-advised-obama-campaign.html?pagewanted=all&_r=0.**

4. Ibid.

Chapter 8

1. Taylor, E. 2009. *Mind Programming: From Persuasion and Brainwashing to Self-Help and Practical Metaphysics.* Carlsbad, CA: Hay House.

2. McTaggart, L. 2001. *The Field: The Quest for the Secret Force of the Universe.* New York: HarperCollins.

3. Taylor, E. 1988. *Subliminal Learning: An Eclectic Approach.* Medical Lake, WA: R. K. Books.

4. Boston University. 2005. "Boston University Psychologists Find Neurological Mechanism for Subliminal Learning." **www.brightsurf.com.**

Chapter 9

1. Mill, J. S. 1961. *Essential Works of John Stuart Mill: Utilitarianism, Autobiography, On Liberty, The Utility of Religion.* Edited by Max Lerner. New York: Bantam Books.

2. Jampolsky, G. 1979. *Love Is Letting Go of Fear.* Berkeley, CA: Celestial Arts.

Chapter 10

1. Adams, S. C., and Kiefer, M. "Testing The Attentional Boundary Conditions of Subliminal Semantic Priming: The Influence of Semantic and Phonological Task

Sets" *Front Hum Neurosci.* 2012; 6: 241. **http://www.ncbi.nlm.nih.gov/pmc/ articles/PMC3430011/.**

2. Taylor, E. 1990. *Subliminal Communication: Emperor's Clothes of Panacea.* 2nd ed. Medical Lake, WA: R. K. Books.

3. Taylor, E. 1995. *Thinking Without Thinking: Who's in Control of Your Mind?* Medical Lake, WA: R. K. Books.

4. Epley, N. 1999. "What Every Skeptic Should Know about Subliminal Persuasion." *Skeptical Inquirer.* Sept–Oct.

5. Bornstein, R. F., and Masling, J. M. 1998. *Empirical Perspectives on the Psychoanalytic Unconscious.* Washington, D.C.: American Psychological Association.

6. Ellis, A. 1988. *How to Stubbornly Refuse to Make Yourself Miserable about Anything (Yes, Anything).* New York: Lyle Stuart.

7. Wolman, B. B. 1973. *Handbook of General Psychology.* Englewood Cliffs, NJ: Prentice Hall.

Chapter 11

1. Massachusetts General Hospital. 2012. "Meditation Appears To Produce Enduring Changes In Emotional Processing in the Brain." Press Release. **http://www .sciencedaily.com/releases/2012/11/121112150339.htm** and **http://www .massgeneral.org/about/pressrelease.aspx?id=1520**

Chapter 12

1. Bower, B. 1993. "Neanderthal Neck Bone Sparks Cross Talk (Hyoid Fossil May Indicate Capacity for Speech)." *Science News,* page 262.

2. Hauser, M., and Andersson, K. 1994. "Experiments and Observation on Vocal Communication and Acoustic Perception in Captive Cotton-top Tamarins and Vervet Monkeys." *Science News,* May 21, page 333.

3. Rossi, E. 1993. *Psychobiology of Mind-Body Healing: New Concepts of Therapeutic Hypnosis.* New York: W. W. Norton and Company.

4. Lipkin, R. 1994. "Simulated Creatures Evolve and Learn." *Science News.* 146. July 23, page 63.

5. Laszlo, E. 1994. "The 'Genius Hypothesis.'" *Journal of Scientific Exploration.* 8, no. 2, 257–67.

6. Weiss, P. 1999. "On the Origin of Circuits." *Science News.* 156, Sept. 4, page 156.

7. Sheldrake, R. 1995. *The Presence of the Past: Morphic Resonance and the Habits of Nature.* Rochester, VT: Park Street Press.

8. Hagelin, J. S., Rainforth, M. V., et al. 1999. "Effects of Group Practice of the Transcendental Meditation Program on Preventing Violent Crime in Washington, DC: Results of the National Demonstration Project June–July 1993." *Social Indicators Research,* 47, 2, 153–201.

9. Schwartz, G. 2002. *The Afterlife Experiments: Breakthrough Scientific Evidence of Life After Death.* New York: Pocket Books.

10. McTaggart, L. 2001. *The Intention Experiment.* London: Harper Element.

11. Taylor, E. 1987. *The Little Black Book.* Medical Lake, WA: R. K. Books.

Chapter 13

1. Krishnamurti, J. 1987. *The Awakening of Intelligence*. New York: Harper & Row.

2. Laing, R. D. 1976. *Politics of Experience*. New York: Ballantine Books.

3. Joseph, R., ed. 2002. *NeuroTheology: Brain, Science, Spirituality, Religious Experience*. San Jose, CA: University Press.

4. Kelley, A. E., and Wang, L. 2012. "A Life Without Lies: Can Living More Honestly Improve Health?" APA 2012 Annual Convention. **http://cbsphilly.files.wordpress .com/2012/08/kelly-a-life-without-lies.pdf**.

5. Boyce, C, et al. 2012. "Is Personality Fixed? Personality Changes as Much as 'Variable' Economic Factors and More Strongly Predicts Changes to Life Satisfaction." *Social Indicators Research* (doi: 10.1007/s11205-012-0006-z) and **http://www.sciencedaily.com/releases/2012/03/120305081412.htm**.

Chapter 14

1. Kanai, R.; Feilden, T.; Firth, C.; and Rees, G. 2011. "Political Orientations Are Correlated with Brain Structure in Young Adults." *Current Biology*. DOI: 10.1016/j.cub.2011.03.017 and **http://www.sciencedaily.com/ releases/2011/04/110407121337.htm**.

2. Bach, R. 1976. *Jonathan Livingston Seagull: A Story*. New York: Avon Books.

Chapter 16

1. Foundation for Inner Peace. 1996. *A Course in Miracles*. New York: Viking.

2. Wilde, S. 1998. *"Life Was Never Meant to Be a Struggle."* Carlsbad, CA: Hay House.

◉◉◉◉◉◉◉

ACKNOWLEDGMENTS

I am indebted, as usual, to my lovely wife for both her encouragement and her perseverance in assisting the editing process. Thank you, Ravinder. I would also like to thank Suzanne Brady, for her extensive editing and reediting, and the Hay House team, especially Patrick Gabrysiak for his invaluable insights.

Over the years, especially during times of controversy, there have been special people who have served almost as my living angels. To them—especially Roy, Lois, and Pat—words cannot adequately express my appreciation.

I am also indebted to the many who have gone before me and whom I cite as inspiring and leading me in my own development.

I acknowledge the thousands who have written me to offer their thanks for my work that has made a difference in their lives. I cannot express in words just how meaningful these notes and letters are to me.

It is important that I acknowledge a wonderful lady who shared a truly life-shaping experience with me—thank you, Connie.

Finally, thank you, each of you, for reading this work.

❁❁❁❁❁

ABOUT THE AUTHOR

Eldon Taylor has made a lifelong study of the human mind and has earned doctoral degrees in psychology and metaphysics. He is a Fellow with the American Psychotherapy Association (APA) and an interdenominational minister.

Eldon was a practicing criminalist for over ten years while completing his education. He supervised and conducted investigations and testing to detect deception. His earliest work with changing inner beliefs was conducted from this setting, including a double-blind study conducted at the Utah State Prison from 1986 to 1987. Eldon is president and director of Progressive Awareness Research, Inc. For more than 25 years, his books, audio and video programs, lectures, and radio and television appearances have approached personal empowerment from the cornerstone perspective of forgiveness, gratitude, and respect for all life. Eldon now lives in the countryside of Washington State with his wife and their two sons. Apart from his family and work, his true passion is horses.

●◉●

Visit Eldon's Website

If you enjoyed this book and would like to learn more about the tools suggested to help you become the person you were meant to be, visit Eldon's websites at **www.eldontaylor.com** and **www .innertalk.com**.

●◉●

InnerTalk Distribution

U.S.A. and Canada
Progressive Awareness Research, Inc.
PO Box 1139
Medical Lake, WA 99022
1 800 964 3551
1 509 299 3377
www.innertalk.com (English)
www.dialogointerno.com (Spanish)

U.K.
Kiki Ltd.
Unit 4, Aylsham Business Estate
Shepheards Close
Aylsham
Norwich
NR11 6SZ
Tel: 01263 738 663
**http://www.kiki-health.co.uk/
products_innertalk.asp**

Germany
Axent Verlag
Steinerne Furt 78
86167 Augsburg
Germany
011 49 821 70 5011
www.axent-verlag.de

Malaysia/Singapore/Brunei
Progressive Awareness Sdn Bhd
2–2 Jalan Pju 8/5E, Perdana Bus. Cntr.
Bandar Damansara Perdana,
47820 Petaling Jaya
Selangor, Malaysia
011 60 37 729 4745
www.innertalk-au.com

Taiwan and China
Easy MindOpen
3F, No. 257, Ho-Ping East Rd. Sec. 2
Taipei, Taiwan, R.O.C
011 886 (227) 010–468(1)
www.iamone.com.tw

Spanish
InnerTalk programs in Spanish can be
obtained from:
www.dialogointerno.com

⁕⊛⁕

Distribution Inquiries
For information regarding distributing
InnerTalk programs, please contact:

Progressive Awareness Research, Inc.
PO Box 1139
Medical Lake, WA 99022
1 800 964 3551
1 509 299 3377
www.innertalk.com

Hay House Titles of Related Interest

YOU CAN HEAL YOUR LIFE, the movie, starring Louise L. Hay & Friends
(available as a 1-DVD program and an expanded 2-DVD set)
Watch the trailer at: **www.LouiseHayMovie.com**

THE SHIFT, the movie,
starring Dr. Wayne W. Dyer
(available as a 1-DVD program and an expanded 2-DVD set)
Watch the trailer at: **www.DyerMovie.com**

●◉●

ALL IS WELL: Heal Your Body with Medicine, Affirmations, and Intuition,
by Louise L. Hay and Mona Lisa Schulz, M.D., Ph.D.

MIND OVER MEDICINE: Scientific Proof That You Can Heal Yourself,
by Lissa Rankin, M.D.

*SOUL LESSONS AND SOUL PURPOSE: A Channeled Guide to
Why You Are Here,* by Sonia Choquette

WHAT TO DO WHEN YOU DON'T KNOW WHAT TO DO,
by Wyatt Webb

VIRUS OF THE MIND: The New Science of the Meme, by Richard Brodie

All of the above are available at your local bookstore,
or may be ordered by contacting Hay House (see next page).

●◉●

We hope you enjoyed this Hay House book. If you'd like to receive our online catalog featuring additional information on Hay House books and products, or if you'd like to find out more about the Hay Foundation, please contact:

Hay House, Inc., P.O. Box 5100, Carlsbad, CA 92018-5100
(760) 431-7695 or (800) 654-5126
(760) 431-6948 (fax) or (800) 650-5115 (fax)
www.hayhouse.com® • **www.hayfoundation.org**

⚫◉⚫

Published and distributed in Australia by: Hay House Australia Pty. Ltd., 18/36 Ralph St., Alexandria NSW 2015 • *Phone:* 612-9669-4299 *Fax:* 612-9669-4144 • www.hayhouse.com.au

Published and distributed in the United Kingdom by: Hay House UK, Ltd., Astley House, 33 Notting Hill Gate, London W11 3JQ • *Phone:* 44-20-3675-2450 *Fax:* 44-20-3675-2451 • www.hayhouse.co.uk

Published and distributed in the Republic of South Africa by: Hay House SA (Pty), Ltd., P.O. Box 990, Witkoppen 2068 • *Phone/Fax:* 27-11-467-8904 www.hayhouse.co.za

Published in India by: Hay House Publishers India, Muskaan Complex, Plot No. 3, B-2, Vasant Kunj, New Delhi 110 070 • *Phone:* 91-11-4176-1620 *Fax:* 91-11-4176-1630 • www.hayhouse.co.in

Distributed in Canada by: Raincoast, 9050 Shaughnessy St., Vancouver, B.C. V6P 6E5 • *Phone:* (604) 323-7100 • *Fax:* (604) 323-2600 • www.raincoast.com

⚫◉⚫

Take Your Soul on a Vacation

Visit **www.HealYourLife.com®** to regroup, recharge, and reconnect with your own magnificence. Featuring blogs, mind-body-spirit news, and life-changing wisdom from Louise Hay and friends.

Visit **www.HealYourLife.com** today!